Conservation of Historic Timber Structures

Butterworth-Heinemann Series in Conservation and Museology

Conservation of Historic Timber Structures

An ecological approach

Knut Einar Larsen
Nils Marstein

OXFORD   AUCKLAND   BOSTON   JOHANNESBURG   MELBOURNE   NEW DELHI

Butterworth-Heinemann
Linacre House, Jordan Hill, Oxford OX2 8DP
225 Wildwood Avenue, Woburn, MA 01801-2041
A division of Reed Educational and Professional Publishing Ltd

 A member of the Reed Elsevier plc group

First published 2000

British Library Cataloguing in Publication Data
A catalogue record for this book is available from the British Library

ISBN 0 7506 3434 0

Library of Congress Cataloguing in Publication Data
A catalogue record for this book is available from the Library of Congress

Composition by Scribe Design, Gillingham, Kent
Printed and bound in Great Britain by The Bath Press, Bath

Contents

Series editors' preface

The conservation of artefacts and buildings has a long history, but the positive emergence of conservation as a profession can be said to date from the foundation of the International Institute for the Conservation of Museum Objects (IIC) in 1950 (the last two words of the title being later changed to Historic and Artistic Works) and the appearance soon after in 1952 of its journal *Studies in Conservation*. The role of the conservator as distinct from those of the restorer and the scientist had been emerging during the 1930s with a focal point in the Fogg Art Museum, Harvard University, which published the precursor to *Studies in Conservation, Technical Studies in the Field of the Fine Arts* (1932–42).

UNESCO, through its Cultural Heritage Division and its publications, had always taken a positive role in conservation and the foundation, under its auspices, of the International Centre for the Study of the Preservation and the Restoration of Cultural Property (ICCROM), in Rome, was a further advance. The Centre was established in 1959 with the aims of advising internationally on conservation problems, co-ordinating conservation activators and establishing standards of training courses.

A significant confirmation of professional progress was the transformation in New York in 1966 of the two committees of the International Council of Museums (ICOM), one curatorial on the Care of Paintings (founded in 1949) and the other mainly scientific (founded in the mid-1950s), into the ICOM Committee for Conservation.

Following the Second International Congress of Architects in Venice in 1964 when the Venice Charter was promulgated, the International Council of Monuments and Sites (ICOMOS) was set up in 1965 to deal with archaeological, architectural and town planning questions, to schedule monuments and sites and to monitor relevant legislation. From the early 1960s onwards, international congresses (and the literature emerging from them) held by IIC, ICOM, ICOMOS and ICCROM not only advanced the subject in its various technical specializations but also emphasized the cohesion of conservators and their subject as an interdisciplinary profession.

The use of the term *Conservation* in the title of this series refers to the whole subject of the care and treatment of valuable artefacts, both movable and immovable, but within the discipline conservation has a meaning which is distinct from that of restoration. *Conservation* used in this specialized sense has two aspects: first, the control of the environment to minimize the decay of artefacts and materials; and, second, their treatment to arrest decay and to stabilize them where possible against further deterioration. Restoration is the continuation of the latter process, when conservation treatment is thought to be insufficient, to the extent of reinstating an object, without falsification, to a condition in which it can be exhibited.

In the field of conservation conflicts of values on aesthetic, historical, or technical grounds are often inevitable. Rival attitudes and methods inevitably arise in a subject which is still developing and at the core of these differences there is often a deficiency of technical knowledge. That is one of the principal *raisons d'être* of this series. In most of these matters ethical principles are the subject of much discussion, and generalizations cannot easily cover (say) buildings, furniture, easel paintings and waterlogged wooden objects.

A rigid, universally agreed principle is that all treatment should be adequately documented. There is also general agreement that structural and decorative falsification should be avoided. In addition there are three other principles which, unless there are overriding objections, it is generally agreed should be followed.

The first is the principle of the reversibility of processes, which states that a treatment should normally be such that the artefact can, if desired, be returned to its pre-treatment condition even after a long lapse of time. This principle is impossible to apply in some cases, for example where the survival of an artefact may depend upon an irreversible process. The second, intrinsic to the whole subject, is that as far as possible decayed parts of an artefact should be conserved and not replaced. The third is that the consequences of the ageing of the original materials (for example 'patina') should not normally be disguised or removed. This includes a secondary proviso that later accretions should not be retained under the false guise of natural patina.

The authors of the volumes in this series give their views on these matters, where relevant, with reference to the types of material within their scope. They take into account the differences in approach to artefacts of essentially artistic significance and to those in which the interest is primarily historical, archaeological or scientific.

The volumes are unified by a systematic and balanced presentation of theoretical and practical material with, where necessary, an objective comparison of different methods and approaches. A balance has also been maintained between the fine (and decorative) arts, archaeology and architecture in those cases where the respective branches of the subject have common ground, for example in the treatment of stone and glass and in the control of the museum environment. Since the publication of the first volume it has been decided to include within the series related monographs and technical studies. To reflect this enlargement of its scope the series has been renamed the Butterworth–Heinemann Series in Conservation and Museology.

Though necessarily different in details of organization and treatment (to fit the particular requirements of the subject) each volume has the same general standard, which is that of such training courses as those of the University of London Institute of Archaeology, the Victoria and Albert Museum, the Conservation Center, New York University, the Institute of Advanced Architectural Studies, York, and ICCROM.

The authors have been chosen from among the acknowledged experts in each field, but as a result of the wide areas of knowledge and technique covered even by the specialized volumes in this series, in many instances multi-authorship has been necessary.

With the existence of IIC, ICOM, ICOMOS and ICCROM, the principles and practice of conservation have become as internationalized as the problems. The collaboration of Consultant Editors will help to ensure that the practices discussed in this series will be applicable throughout the world.

Preface

Through our work with the ICOMOS International Wood Committee, we have had the opportunity to meet colleagues from all over the world and to discuss problems related to the conservation and repair of historic timber structures, often in situ. We have come to realise that there is in fact no single way, but rather several approaches which must be accepted if we are to take a world-wide view on the problems of preservation of historic timber structures. There are no standard technical solutions that can be applied universally. Our experience is that repair approaches must be geared towards the specific cultural, architectural and environmental challenges in the country or region where the historic timber structure is located.

With this background, one of our most important tasks on the Wood Committee has been the development of the Principles for the Preservation of Historic Timber Structures, upon which this book is based. We wish to thank our colleagues on the Wood Committee for the inspiring and illuminating discussions we have had together over the years which have led to the development of the Principles. We would also like to thank our colleagues at ICCROM (International Centre for the Study and the Preservation and Restoration of Cultural Property) and the lecturers and participants in UNESCO's International Courses on Wood Conservation Technology whom we met between 1984 and 1996 when we directed this training programme. They gave us valuable input in the development of the Principles and contributed to our understanding of the global problems connected with the preservation of historic timber structures. In particular, we wish to thank those of our colleagues from the Wood Committee and further afield who have given us examples used in this book.

It is a particular challenge to write a book in a language that is not your own. Therefore, we wish to extend our heartfelt thanks to our friend and colleague Ingrid Greenhow. When she lived in Norway, she worked with us in the organisation of the UNESCO International Course on Wood Conservation Technology in 1986 and 1988. Since returning to England, she has continued to advise us on the use of language and to proof-read our professional papers. She has given us valuable advice and fresh perspectives in the development of the manuscript, in addition to helping us with questions of language.

The material on Japan in this book is adapted from *Architectural Preservation in Japan* (Larsen, 1994).

We thank all those who have given us permission to reproduce drawings and photographs. They are acknowledged in the individual figure legends. Those illustrations for which a source is not acknowledged were drawn or photographed by the authors.

Introduction

This book offers a new and sustainable approach to the preservation of historic timber structures. It is geared towards a world-wide view of preservation problems relating to timber structures from a cultural perspective. We aim to introduce ideas and solutions that may be universal in their scope, while respecting cultural diversity.

This book is not designed as a handbook. In the view of the authors, specific repair techniques must be adapted to the particular conditions and available resources of each country or region. In this way, the authors wish to respect the diversity of cultures, the types of timber structures and the particular requirements of the various environments where they are located. The necessity for this approach is discussed further in Chapter 3. Most countries have their own handbooks, publications or training courses which will introduce typical technical solutions suitable for their own particular culture and technical preservation problems relating to timber structures. Examples are English Heritage and the Association for Preservation Technology in the USA and Canada. There is also an extensive amount of literature on this subject, including Charles (1984) and Weaver (1993).

What we regard as universal in preservation thinking are some basic ideas concerning the values of cultural properties and how these best can be maintained through repair work. While particular techniques must necessarily be adapted to local conditions, we wish to introduce globally applicable ways of thinking. The ideas we present here are based on ideas developed within the framework of the International Wood Committee of ICOMOS (International Council on Monuments and Sites).

1 Using the wisdom of previous generations in repair work

Based on the Wood Committee's *Principles for the Preservation of Historic Timber Structures*, the main thesis of this book is that when we carry out preservation work or repair timber structures from the past, we should duplicate, as far as this is possible, the choices that previous generations made, out of respect for their insight, wisdom and knowledge. This means that:

1. when replacement of a member in a timber structure is necessary, replacement timber of the same species of wood and of a similar quality should be used;
2. tools and techniques identical or similar to those used by previous generations of craftsmen to convert and dress the timber and to assemble the various members should be used.

(a)

(b)

Figure 1   (a) The David B. Gamble house, Pasadena, USA: architects Charles and Henry Greene, 1908. (b) Detail of veranda

The reason for this approach is that it is the insight, wisdom and knowledge of previous generations as represented in the structure handed down to us that constitute the authentic historic document. It is out of respect for the human thinking and work inherent in this authentic document that we try to honour previous generations by duplicating their choices and endeavours. In this way, the beauty intended by the creator of the original structure can be retained. Only in cases where the original choices have not proved to be durable or sustainable should we opt for modern solutions.

2 An ecological approach to preservation

It is this approach – which has its roots in respect for the crafts and craftsmanship – which is the essential aspect of what we call an ecological approach to preservation. This is the main theme of the book, which is discussed in detail in Chapters 1, 2, 5 and 10. By an ecological approach we mean, moreover, that historic timber structures must be regarded as being more than isolated objects where the sole purpose is to conserve the historic substance or fabric. We regard historic timber structures as sources of inspiration and living evidence of methods of sustainable building practices and knowledge of materials, which could well be adapted to the repair of the same structures, as well as to contemporary building practice.

An ecological approach, in our view, also includes an environmentally responsible approach to limiting the use of toxic substances to preserve wood from decay and for repair, such as epoxies, which we do not recommend. This is discussed in Chapters 4 and 9. A main theme is that minimum intervention in a structure is the best policy, and that preventive conservation should always

have first priority. This is the subject of Chapter 7. The central aspect of the ecological approach is to try to understand the knowledge of previous generations concerning the use of forests and the use of timber in structures in order to make them durable. This aspect is discussed throughout the book, but in particular in Chapters 6 and 8.

3 Timber and forests

Wood as an organic material may decay and degrade rapidly compared to stone, brick or other major historic building materials, as a result of moisture, fungi, insect attack or fire. Wood is actively affected by relative humidity, which causes it to expand and contract. Moreover, wood may be deformed by warping. Defects in wooden structural members, whether at the joints or elsewhere, are more critical to a structure's load-bearing capacity than other primary building materials. The big difference between stone and wood is the time dimension in the ageing process. The stage where wood rots may come a hundred or a thousand times faster than the stage at which stone is reduced to gravel. The ageing and deterioration of wood is more rapid and is also of a different character than that of stone: in stone, the deterioration moves from the outside towards the inside; in wood, decay and deterioration caused by fungi and insects may start from within and move outwards. These characteristics necessitate various interventions in historic timber structures in order to preserve them, which are different from those used in structures constructed of more permanent materials.

A main argument of this book is that the preservation of historic timber structures starts in the forest and thus it establishes a link between cultural heritage preservation and the conservation and sustainable use of forest resources. Public interest and concern for the health and well-being of the world's forests, the natural resource for wood, have never been greater than today, following the United Nations Conference on Environment and Development in Rio de Janeiro in 1992. This book argues for and demonstrates the close relationship that exists between the preservation of timber structures and the sustainable use of the world's forest resources.

4 ICOMOS, the International Wood Committee and the Wood Committee's Principles

In today's heritage conservation thinking, increasing attention has been focused on respect for cultural and heritage diversity. Too much diversity and tolerance leads to there being little that is a common denominator, and we therefore argue for the necessity of an overruling norm for the preservation of the world's cultural heritage made of wood. Our thinking is based on international preservation doctrine, such as the Venice Charter, the Nara Document on Authenticity, and, in particular, the *Principles for the Preservation of Historic Timber Structures*, adopted by the ICOMOS International Wood Committee.

ICOMOS is an international non-governmental organisation of professionals, dedicated to the conservation of the world's historic monuments and sites. ICOMOS provides a forum for professional dialogue and a vehicle for the collection, evaluation and dissemination of information on conservation principles, techniques and policies. The organisation was founded in 1965, as a result of the international adoption of the Charter for the Conservation and Restoration of Monuments and Sites (the Venice Charter) the preceding year. ICOMOS is UNESCO's principal adviser in matters concerning the conservation and protection of monuments and sites. Today the organisation has national committees in nearly 90 countries. The Wood Committee is one of the sixteen ICOMOS international scientific committees of experts from around the world. Through these committees, ICOMOS seeks to establish international standards for the preservation, restoration and management of the cultural environment.

Ever since the Wood Committee was established in 1975, the need for a set of preservation principles has been a continuous theme in the Committee's deliberations and activities. The current Principles are based on proposals by Sir Bernard Feilden (1984) and Michael Mennim (1988). The Principles were debated at the meetings and international symposia of the Wood Committee in Nepal in 1992, Japan in 1994, Bulgaria in 1996, England in 1997 and in China in 1998. In addition, the Wood Committee has continuously sought the advice of both its members and experts outside the Committee in the development of the Principles. The Committee therefore believes that the current version represents the predominant view among the world's experts on the preservation of historic timber structures.

Based on the ICOMOS Wood Committee's Principles, the purpose of this book is to introduce basic and universally-applicable principles and practices for the protection and preservation of historic timber structures with due respect for their cultural significance. Historic timber structures, as defined in the Wood Committee's Principles and in this book, are all types of buildings or constructions wholly or partially in timber which are of cultural significance or which form constituent parts of an historic area.

The book addresses students, craftsmen and professionals who are involved or who have an interest in the protection and preservation of historic timber structures: architects, conservators, engineers, craftsmen and site managers. It will also be of interest to members of the public who wish to develop their knowledge of the preservation of the world's wooden cultural heritage, as well as those who are interested in building practices that may be compatible with sustainable development.

1

The sustainability of traditional materials and craftsmanship

The world of international preservation thinking seemed less complicated in the 1960s when Europe, and in particular European stone and masonry building traditions, formed the basis from which modern preservation theory has evolved. Today, the recommendations of the international preservation bodies have to take into account the phenomenon of globalisation and the increasing awareness of the legitimate right of cultures to express their own values through the preservation of their cultural heritage. Yesterday's truths are no longer necessarily valid.

The Nara Conference on Authenticity, held in Nara, Japan, in 1995, illustrates this new situation very well. The conference was organised jointly by UNESCO, ICOMOS, ICCROM and the Japanese Agency for Cultural Affairs with the aim of clarifying the 'test of authenticity' in relation to UNESCO's World Heritage Convention (Larsen, 1995). It brought together forty-five of the leading experts in the field of preservation of cultural properties. In all, they represented international organisations, twenty-six countries from around the world and all the major cultural regions and building traditions of the world. The conference adopted a declaration entitled the *Nara Document on Authenticity*. The Nara Document reflects the fact that international preservation doctrine has moved from a Eurocentric approach to a postmodern position, characterised by the recognition of cultural relativism.

The Nara Document encourages preservation experts to clarify the use of the concept of authenticity within their own countries and cultural spheres. Only then can they engage their colleagues from other parts of the world in an open dialogue on the understanding that the search for authenticity is universal, but recognising that the ways and means to preserve the authenticity of cultural heritage are culturally dependent. The basic message of the Nara Document is that the world's immense diversity of cultures and types of heritage should be respected. No one has the right to force a preconceived system of values and ideas for cultural heritage preservation on any nation or culture.

Nonetheless, the Nara Document reaffirms the most basic document in international preservation thinking, the 'Venice Charter' of 1964. The Venice Charter was adopted as a resolution by the second International Congress of Architects and Technicians of Historic Monuments in Venice in 1964 (Larsen, 1994: 1). From its conception, the charter has been continuously criticised for being Eurocentric and for not taking into consideration different building materials. Nevertheless, the Venice Charter remains the only accepted base of thinking for preservation experts all over the world, and reference is constantly made to it. It looks as though the

Venice Charter will retain this pre-eminent status well into the twenty-first century. The reason for the acceptance and widespread use of the Venice Charter is that the text is open to interpretation, so that widely differing solutions to preservation problems may be chosen and yet still claim to be in accordance with the Venice Charter.

The preservation ideologies upon which international recommendations are based are derived from buildings made of stone, rather than wood. For example, the Venice Charter was conceived by experts who drew their experience mainly from work with stone buildings. As a consequence, Article 11 of the Charter refers to issues that are particularly relevant to stone buildings, as, for example, 'the superimposed work of different periods' which should be respected and 'the revealing of the underlying state', which can only be justified in exceptional circumstances. Accordingly, such terms require interpretation in order to be applied to timber buildings. In general terms, the changes which have taken place in stone or brick buildings during their history are basically characterised by the addition of new parts and new layers, for instance, new layers of plaster. In the timber building tradition, changes are characterised by the replacement of members, which may have decayed due to fungi or insect attack, or been destroyed by fire. As long as we speak of the preservation of historical strata, the theory can only be relevant for timber buildings if we also include replaced members in the concept of strata.

As early as the Congress in Venice in 1964, serious objections were raised against the universal applicability of the Venice Charter. The United States delegation saw the Charter as dealing principally with the preservation of stone buildings, common in Europe, but a topic of less interest in the United States, where construction is primarily of wood and other materials (Stipe, 1990: 407). When

ICOMOS summed up twenty-five years of experience with the Venice Charter in 1990, several ICOMOS national committees and individual experts shared the US Committee's concern that the Charter, while being of a culturally limited scope, is also too general to be applied to meeting the needs of different architectural, political and economic situations, as well as widely differing architectural techniques and building materials (Stipe, 1990: 415; ICOMOS, 1990: 33–6). In particular, historic buildings and monuments built partly or wholly of wood present special problems in preservation. This is why the ICOMOS Wood Committee has developed its Principles.

1.1 The ICOMOS International Wood Committee's *Principles for the Preservation of Historic Timber Structures*

The preamble to the Wood Committee's Principles affirms that timber structures from all periods are important as part of the cultural heritage of the world. The Principles consider the great diversity of historic timber structures and also the various species and qualities of wood used to build them. One of the members of the ICOMOS Wood Committee, Fred Charles, a leading UK conservation architect of timber structures, has proposed that there are as many ways of building with timber as there are species of trees, differences in climate and contrasts of terrain (Charles, 1984: 10). This may indeed represent a tremendous challenge for those who aim to consider all these differences and the diversity in cultures, and then recommend an approach to the preservation of timber structures that may be applied universally. For example, a total of 30 000 angiosperm (hardwood) and 520 gymnosperm (softwood) tree species are recognised. We can safely conclude that natural diversity is immense and almost beyond our comprehension.

There are great differences of opinion between experts on the preservation of timber structures in different countries concerning the 'best' or most suitable preservation methods. Even within the same country, experts may hold widely differing opinions on the best way to preserve their national heritage resources made of wood. Some say that the material is sacred and every effort must be made to save every bit of historic material, even if it is severely decayed and can no longer perform any structural role. These experts propose reinforcement with plastic, steel and even concrete (Salaün, 1995). In the view of the authors of this book, experience shows that we have to relearn the traditional knowledge of materials and construction techniques in order to help our monuments to survive.

However, we do not reject technological progress. The Wood Committee's Principles, like Article 10 of the Venice Charter, accept the use of contemporary materials, such as polymeric materials, and techniques such as structural steel reinforcement in preservation or repair work. However, the Principles emphasise that such materials and techniques must be chosen and used with the greatest caution, and only in cases where the durability and structural behaviour of the materials and construction techniques have been satisfactorily proven over a sufficiently long period of time. This view is, we believe, shared by most specialists (see for example Brereton, 1995: 4).

1.1.1 The Wood Committee's Principles: the use of traditional methods

The main message of the Principles, however, is that traditional methods should,

wherever possible, always be followed in repair work. We should look at the possibility of preserving or repairing a timber structure using techniques and construction technology which correspond to those used originally. This also includes the use of the traditional dressing tools or machinery. For example, the Principles advise that when a part of a member is replaced, traditional woodwork joints should be used to splice the new part to the existing part, if this is appropriate and compatible with structural requirements.

Article 10 of the Venice Charter seems somewhat inadequate in propagating traditional techniques in preservation work, although it expresses concern for the structural behaviour and durability of modern materials:

> *Where traditional techniques prove inadequate, the consolidation of a monument can be achieved by the use of any modern technique for conservation and construction, the efficacy of which has been shown by scientific data and proved by experience.*

Harald Langberg, a Danish architectural historian and one of the co-signers of the Venice Charter in 1964, explains the background. It was taken for granted that the same materials and techniques which were used during the previous construction work on the building should also be used in the preservation work. On the other hand, in cases where traditional materials and techniques had proved to be unserviceable, one should not be committed to repeating the mistakes of the past. This scepticism towards contemporary materials was based on an awareness that these might solve a specific technical problem, but might also have unforeseen side effects which could cause serious problems in the future (Langberg, 1975: 17).

Traditional methods of repair of timber buildings presuppose:

1. the availability of timber of the same species, grading and scantling as the old, decayed timber which is to be replaced;
2. that forest owners are interested in keeping forest reserves with old-growth, 'mature' trees;
3. the availability of craftsmen, in particular carpenters who are familiar with the handling of traditional tools; and
4. the availability of traditional tools.

In addition, conservation architects, and, ideally, carpenters as well, should have a thorough knowledge of traditional design methods and construction techniques. It is an accepted fact in today's industrial societies that it is extremely difficult to fulfil all these conditions, or even a few of them.

Advocating the use of traditional materials and techniques in repair work is, however, not particularly radical. Indeed, this approach has been used by Japanese preservation experts for nearly a century; in the UK, the Society for the Protection of Ancient Buildings (SPAB) and English Heritage advocate that, wherever possible, repairs to structural timbers should be carried out in timber using traditional carpentry methods (Boutwood, 1991: 5). In Germany, leading experts advocate the use of traditional techniques in timber-framed buildings (Gerner, 1979: 76). In the Scandinavian countries, traditional methods are not only preferred but are dominant in the preservation and repair of historic timber structures. In other countries, the situation is quite different. Sometimes we see that a wish to elevate the repair of timber structures to the realm of 'science' leads to neglect of traditional repair methods in carpentry techniques, in the belief that the use of modern materials is more 'scientific'.

Figure 1.1 The Church of the Transfiguration on the island of Kizhi, Lake Onega, the Karelian Russian Republic, completed in 1714. The Kizhi Pogost World Heritage Site includes the Church of the Transfiguration, the Church of the Virgin of the Intercession (1764), a bell-tower (1861) and the fences, which were reconstructed in 1959. The log structure of the Church of the Transfiguration shows the Russian architect's extravagant ideas and how a carpenter could push his techniques to their furthest limits. Today, the church is in urgent need of repair. The material and structural decay is so severe that the idea of dismantling the church completely was put to the ICOMOS Wood Committee in 1988. As yet, no decision has been made regarding the restoration of this structure, which is of supreme national and international significance. The Wood Committee strongly argues the case for minimum intervention and maximum retention of existing materials wherever possible, using traditional carpentry techniques in the repair work. (Photo by Sjur Helseth, Directorate for Cultural Heritage, Norway)

Figure 1.2 A carpenter's axe used for *sprett-telgjing*

1.2 The need for skilled carpenters

The need to use modern materials in repair work may also result from the lack of competent craftsmen. When the cry for skilled craftsmen is raised in international conferences and meetings, one almost always thinks of artistically oriented craftsmen, such as stone sculptors and wood carvers. The lack of ordinary construction workers is rarely regarded as a problem. This is because construction techniques have been regarded with less interest than the architectural surfaces. Moreover, construction work is often seen as low-status work where you more or less can pick people from the street and put them to work. Construction work is not regarded as something for which particular competence is required.

In Scandinavia the situation is somewhat better, with construction workers with an independent attitude, well trained and relatively well paid, quick, ambitious and with a willingness to learn. As a result, training such carpenters for repair work situations can be a rewarding experience for everyone concerned. In the countries or regions where traditional repair methods predominate, the work of the craftsmen is also respected. This respect for the knowledge and experience of carpenters and other craftsmen is, in our view, a necessary prerequisite for successful preservation work.

To understand the craftsmen and their techniques which produced the heritage we now need to preserve, we need to see the buildings from the perspective of those who built them, and base our interpretations on the limitations and possibilities of the technical knowledge and capabilities of previous generations as represented, for example, by their tools. To do this, we need to work closely with carpenters who are the only people with the necessary competence to analyse the traces of tools on the original surfaces.

An example of this is a specific North European medieval carpentry technique used to finish the surface of exposed timbers in log buildings, known as *sprett-telgjing* in Norwegian. When Norwegian carpenters tried to reconstruct the technique in the early 1990s, they used axes or adzes of all shapes and sizes until they discovered that the technique used in medieval Norwegian carpentry was still being used in Northern Russia. The Norwegians noticed that Russian carpenters used an ordinary axe, which was also used for a number of other purposes. They then realised that medieval Norwegian carpenters probably did not possess large tool chests with a lot of specialist tools. The medieval carpenters may well have had just a few tools, and an axe or adze, for example, would have been used for a variety of operations or purposes. In other words, the carpenters of the 1990s had to think 'medieval' in order to understand the practice of the technique.

1.3 Traditional materials and traditional crafts as cultural heritage

We would like to argue that traditional materials and traditional crafts must be regarded as a part of cultural heritage. Furthermore, we believe that preservation requires traditional materials that can function

with the building technically, aesthetically and historically. By 'traditional building materials' we mean materials that have been used over a period of time and which are rooted in past local or regional building activity. Most of these materials were extracted directly from nature, such as wood or stone, and often the processing or finishing of the materials was carried out on the building site by the craftsmen who built the house or structure. The knowledge of the properties of the materials was based on experience inherited from previous generations.

Previously, people regarded building materials for what they were. They knew that some materials or some parts of a buildings or structure deteriorated faster than others, and that these materials or parts required more frequent repair work. Seasonal bad weather may have accelerated the deterioration. This was accepted as a fact of life. Today, we still have the same knowledge, but we no longer accept the realities. Contractors are forced to sign contracts that guarantee the durability of their work. Consequently they are sometimes forced to reinforce traditional materials.

Northern Europe departed from a thousand-year-long building tradition during the 1950s. This tradition was based on well-proven materials, techniques and building systems. Since then, we have had some fifty years of new techniques and new materials that may last a mere ten years. In addition, many of these new materials, such as asbestos and particleboard, have been shown to cause allergies and increase the risk of cancer (Hidemark, 1994). In 1900, some fifty different building materials were in use in Norway. Almost a century later, there are more than 40 000 different materials. Many of them did not exist ten years ago; many of them will probably not exist ten years from now.

The strength of the traditional building materials lies in the fact that they are well tested, often over centuries. This should be a sufficient guarantee of their reliability and durability. No two- or ten-year guarantee is required for these materials. Correctly produced, processed and finished, and correctly used in the building or structure, they are indeed the only materials that an old building or structure needs. A serious comparison of the durability criteria of older building technology and present technology would be fruitful. Modern technology is based on the assumption that the buildings will be written off in thirty years' time. This is the modern durability perspective, but is this really what people want? Our proposal that traditional means of repair work should be tried first is not about a romantic relationship with traditional or ancient building technology; nor is it an attempt to turn back the clock. It is about a rational evaluation of what was once considered to be good, reliable technology. Perhaps the next generation's technology will develop through bringing together restoration and contemporary building technology.

In older buildings there was an ecology of materials, a natural dependence between the building materials to create a balance of strength, movements due to changes in humidity and temperature. In many cases, when we add new materials, the balance that once existed between traditional materials is distorted or destroyed. Many people, including contractors, combine materials uncritically. Perhaps the time allocated for project preparation and construction is so short today that we are not able to evaluate our proposals properly?

In a wider perspective, this leads to the question of reparability, to the problem of future maintenance. We should plan and build in order to decrease the maintenance problems for the future. In this context, traditional building technology was good. It was based on centuries of testing, in contrast to

modern laboratory tests, often carried out by the manufacturers themselves.

Finally, there is the criterion of ageing. Modern houses are not built to age graciously. While historic buildings in traditional materials age with dignity, modern materials rarely seem to have this ability. Gracious ageing may be considered as the most superior quality of the concept of beauty in relation to historic timber structures.

An interesting example of the traditional understanding of the logic and nature of wood can be found in the nineteenth-century boathouses in Nordmøre, Norway. In these buildings, the walls are clapped with pine boards, normally of high quality, though not always heartwood. The boards are of similar thickness, and are nailed towards the upper edge, just below the point where they overlap. Usually, the boards are put up with the backside facing outwards. As a result, the outer edge bends outwards in dry weather and bends inward again with increasing humidity. The wall thus provides a form of natural ventilation, with airing in dry weather and tightening in periods of humidity. In this way, the boarding is preserved. This is a way of understanding materials and building techniques which could be revived in contemporary construction techniques to great benefit.

We are convinced that the future of building preservation lies in the combined preservation of the physical remains of our heritage resources on the one hand, and, on the other, the preservation of the knowledge of the traditional building materials and construction techniques that were used to produce such resources. There is a future potential in revitalising the knowledge of traditional building materials and techniques which will not only benefit historic buildings but also contemporary construction work. Previous generations managed to build timber structures that have in some cases lasted for more

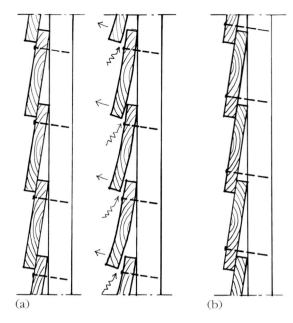

(a)   (b)

Figure 1.3 (a) Traditional wooden panelling in boathouses, Nordmøre, Norway. The boards are nailed towards the upper edge, just below the joint where they overlap. In dry weather, the lower board ends bend outwards, allowing dry air into the construction. In wet weather the boards close again. (b) Modern wooden panelling, Norway. The boards are nailed at the lower end. This ensures weather-tight panelling in all conditions

than a thousand years. We have to conclude that they knew something about wood and construction techniques in wood which has been forgotten today. They knew the qualities of wood far better than many modern architects who sometimes use wood as if it were a dead material, like plastic. The processing or production of traditional building materials, and the execution of many traditional techniques (e.g. jointing), were labour-intensive. With today's wages (in industrialised countries), it is tempting to exchange labour-intensive expensive techniques for modern techniques, in order to save money. Moreover, the supply of most traditional materials is limited and the prices may be high. Modern materials and techniques are generally cheaper. Therefore, it may be a great challenge to motivate a building owner to bear the additional costs of having the repair work done using traditional materials and techniques.

1.4 Revival of lost craft techniques and training programmes

Whether the traditional knowledge is preserved or must be revitalised, comprehensive training programmes on the protection, preservation and conservation of historic timber structures are a fundamental prerequisite for successful preservation. The Wood Committee's Principles add to this that regeneration of values related to the cultural significance of historic timber structures through educational programmes is an essential requisite of a sustainable preservation and development policy. Training programmes should address all relevant professions and trades involved in such work, and, in particular, architects, conservators, engineers, craftsmen and site managers.

It is well worth bearing in mind that knowledge of the traditional techniques of craftsmanship is extremely difficult to revive and retrieve once it is lost. Continuous practice is the only way to preserve such knowledge. However, we are faced with the dilemma that old techniques and working methods and processes have been outmoded and no longer belong to the practical crafts techniques. Knowledge and skills which are no longer in demand cannot survive in trade or business. Knowledge based on tradition that is no longer put into practice rapidly falls into oblivion but may be revived through research and revitalised through training.

Our fundamental challenge then becomes how to revive these lost techniques. The solution to this may be the establishment of a 'core project' such as the programme carried out by the Norwegian Directorate for Cultural Heritage between 1991 and 1996, where a large number of craftsmen were trained on the job, while repairing 250 medieval timber buildings (Haslestad, 1991, 1993a, 1993b). Our experience from this programme is one of the reasons that have convinced us that the approach to the preservation and repair based on historic materials and techniques is to be preferred. We have further been convinced by the experience of our Swedish colleagues (Holmström, 1993; Hidemark, 1994). At the beginning of the 1990s, the Swedish National Board of Antiquities established a project called 'Wood and wooden architecture: materials, building technology, craft techniques and restoration' (Ponnert, 1994; Ponnert and Sjömar, 1993, 1994a, 1994b). The focus of this programme has been on craft and carpentry techniques and the assumption that techniques of craftsmanship must be considered a part of the cultural heritage.

Our most important source of inspiration, however, is Japanese preservation practice, which systematically applies traditional materials and techniques in preservation work. We may, in fact, say that the crux of Japanese preservation is the recognition of the mutual dependence of the preservation of buildings and the preservation of crafts. Through preserving historic buildings, historic techniques of craftsmanship are preserved; and, vice versa, by preserving the historic techniques of craftsmanship, it is possible to preserve historic buildings with compatible materials and in using compatible techniques (Larsen, 1994).

In order to analyse craft techniques and to assimilate knowledge of historic techniques, it is essential that craftsmen and building historians work together. Knowledge that has been carried by tradition must enter the realm of scientific knowledge. It is the craftsmen – the carpenters – who have the 'key' to a really deep understanding of the art of timber construction. An historic building or structure where information about how it was built is lacking should be regarded as incomplete or imperfect heritage.

We should consider living traditions of techniques of craftsmanship and the continuation of human knowledge as having highly important cultural values. We should also consider continuous traditional maintenance as part of the value of an historic timber structure, an important historical tradition that must not be broken. Repeated authentic maintenance should be accepted as an inalienable part of the value of the structure.

1.5 Techniques of craftsmanship and research into architectural history

Our architectural heritage has been built by craftsmen. Therefore, the availability of competent craftsmen will have a significant effect on the approaches to building preservation. Many regard techniques of craftsmanship as purely practical skills. They are not able to see the 'theory' behind all the steps of the working process in the sense that these are adapted to such features as material properties, technical conditions, ergonomics, the mode of operation of tools, form and aesthetics. We may therefore regard the different working techniques as solutions to time- and site-specific building problems. By investigating these aspects, we may obtain information about the society and the era which the building represents.

Wood preserves traces of history. Through our historic timber buildings we have the opportunity to understand history in a way that can never be told by books or written sources. However, this presupposes that we are able to interpret such traces. Knowledge of crafts and techniques then becomes a key to the information carried in the vast files represented by our cultural heritage.

The knowledge of earlier crafts and techniques is carried by tradition. The knowledge and skills are connected with the people who practised them and are transmitted from one generation of craftsmen to the next as part of a tradition. When the tradition is broken, no new experiences are added, but the old ones are gradually diminished or reduced. Thus, the documentation of crafts and techniques is essential. However, the documentation of techniques of craftsmanship has its own methodological problems. It is about the description and analyses of processes, not 'stationary' buildings. Important parts of such knowledge lie, for instance, in the hands, in the body's centre of gravity and in the position of the feet. The training of craftsmen follows directions that are not purely academic. Such knowledge can only partly be verbalised. It is transmitted or transferred through actual work. The teacher or master leads, the student or apprentice follows.

There is a vast resource of knowledge in historic timber structures which only architects, engineers and craftsmen working together can manage to extract. This knowledge may greatly benefit modern building activity and the preservation and repair of the structures which concern us. Our first requirement is, therefore, to respect the work of carpenters for two main reasons; firstly, because they can repair our historic timber structures, and secondly, because only with their help will we be able to extract all possible information from historic constructions and surfaces. Moreover, historic construction practices and building types were generally based on the sustainable use of natural resources. This is also a type of knowledge that is highly necessary in contemporary construction practice. In short, historic timber structures are a knowledge base or resource for contemporary activity.

1.6 Repair and restoration and the quality of wood

The same type of wood should be used in restoration and replacement work as in the original construction. As each species has its own specific physical properties, using the same kind means that the replacement parts will behave in the same way as the original material.

In historic timber structures we can see that wood was treated as a material with great individual variations. This is in contrast to contemporary handling of the material, where wood is reduced to a commercial commodity with uniform properties. The ancient carpenters understood the qualities of wood and they were also able to recognise these qualities in the standing tree. Today, we may be able to provide the timber we need for restoration purposes, but this often forces us to bypass commercial timber traders. This requires knowledge and resources. In important restoration projects, it may even be necessary to select timber from the forests, as was done in days gone by.

The second requirement in implementing a strategy for the repair of timber structures using traditional methods is therefore to have forest resources which can provide timber of a suitable quality. The Wood Committee's Principles encourage the establishment and protection of forest or woodland reserves where appropriate timber can be obtained for the preservation and repair of historic timber structures (see Chapter 6).

In our view, the preservation and repair of timber structures using traditional methods will, firstly, preserve the integrity of the historic buildings and, secondly, revive the ecological thinking which characterised the societies that produced them. To sum up, our aim in architectural preservation is twofold: first, to preserve and repair historic timber structures with compatible materials and technologies, and second, to take an environmentally friendly approach to preservation based on the knowledge and understanding of previous generations of the wonderful qualities of wood.

2

In the full richness of their authenticity

The primary aim of preservation, according to the Wood Committee's Principles, is to maintain the historical integrity of our cultural heritage. Historic buildings should be kept as authentic artefacts that directly link the present with the past. This universal truth may, however, result in widely differing solutions in the form of materials and techniques for the maintenance of the values we attribute to the timber structure in question. Our beliefs, or values, are a kind of blueprint through which we filter the world. They affect our decisions and how we feel about things – they are the building blocks of our perception. One widely held belief is that our historic buildings are 'documents' from the past which should be kept as unaltered as possible, like all historic documents.

The principal reason today why we consider historic buildings worthy of preservation, is that they are primary sources of our knowledge of the era in which they were built. They are, if we have sufficient insight and knowledge to read them, documents from which we may gather knowledge of many aspects of the culture that produced them. This notion was put forward by the Austrian art historian Max Dvorak in 1916. Since the majority of people would consider

it a crime to forge historic documents, it should likewise also be out of the question, according to Dvorak, to make changes to historic buildings so that the 'story' they transmit becomes falsified.

2.1 Aspects of 'authenticity'

The comparison between historic documents and historic buildings with regard to their authenticity is relevant. In fact, the concept of authenticity was originally used by the Graeco-Roman culture as qualifying the texts emanating from the legal and religious authorities (Choay, 1995). The etymology of authenticity is quite straightforward: the word derives from the Greek term *authentikos*, which means 'genuine'.

What then is a 'genuine' or 'authentic' historic building? The process of inscribing an historic building or site in UNESCO's World Heritage List can help us to grasp the significance of the issues or aspects involved in the authenticity or 'genuineness' of an historic building (UNESCO, 1972, 1988). An historic building which is proposed for inclusion in the World Heritage List must meet the *test of authenticity in design, materials, workmanship or setting. (UNESCO, 1988: article 24)*

An historic building is, according to the Venice Charter, 'imbued with a message from the past'. This message, or rather these messages, are past cultural and historical values that are carried by the physical substance, the form and the environment (or setting) of the building. In its substance and form are representations of the technological knowledge and competence of the past. These historical messages must be safeguarded as genuine or authentic historical manifestations.

Confusion often arises in the preservation debate because 'authentic' does not necessarily mean 'original'. In relation to the World Heritage Convention, it is emphasised that the evaluation of authenticity

does not limit consideration to original form and structure but includes all subsequent modifications and additions over the course of time, which themselves possess artistic or historic value. (UNESCO, 1988: article 24)

This understanding of the concept of authenticity is in accordance with Article 11 of the Venice Charter which asserts that

the valid contributions of all periods to the building of a monument must be respected, since unity of style is not the aim of restoration.

Therefore, it is not the original formal concept which is regarded as authentic, but the building as it has been handed down to us through history, with all its modifications and additions due to repair necessitated by decay of the structure and its materials, and by modifications for functional or aesthetic reasons.

The 'test of authenticity' was adopted by the World Heritage Committee in 1977. Since then, the Committee and the state parties to the World Heritage Convention have encountered problems in applying the test. This is due, on the one hand, to the relative vagueness of the concepts involved, and, on the other, to the different cultural interpretations of the concept of authenticity. In 1992, the World Heritage Committee recommended a critical evaluation of the test. This resulted in two conferences being held in 1994 under the auspices of UNESCO, ICOMOS and ICCROM. A preparatory workshop was held in Norway in February 1994 (Larsen and Marstein, 1994b). In November the same year the Nara Conference on Authenticity resulted in the adoption of the *Nara Document on Authenticity* (Larsen, 1995).

The workshop on authenticity in Bergen, Norway in 1994 proposed reconsidering and extending the definitions of the concepts of the present 'test of authenticity' of the Operational Guidelines of the World Heritage Convention. The proposal outlined five areas in which authenticity may be regarded as essential for the truthfulness of the heritage resource in question (Larsen and Marstein, 1994b: 132–133):

1. form or design (form is something that exists, design is intended);
2. material or substance;
3. function or use;
4. context or setting, the spirit of place (*genius loci*); and
5. techniques, traditions or processes, which include pre-industrial as well as industrial techniques and processes.

All international preservation recommendations are based on the idea that the cultural and historical values of historic buildings are directly linked to 'authentic material', the original material substance. All other values are attached to the material value. The materials are carriers of the historical message. In these materials lies the evidence of a lost knowledge, of ideas and ideals. Is, however, the strong focus on the material value of the object (building, building element, the physical substance) correct, relevant or the best or only way to regard values? How do we evaluate a particular woodwork joint in relation to the knowledge required to cut this joint? This has to do with our basic philosophy, our beliefs about what is valuable in life and in our environment.

The suggestion of the international recommendations that authentic materials are the carriers or transmitters of cultural and historical values is based on a European understanding of values. If, for example, we look to Japan, we will find that not only do the historic buildings still exist, but also the knowledge of how they were constructed. The Japanese value both the knowledge of how things are done, and the physical substance.

This is precisely what we have adopted as the main argument of this book: preservation and the implementation in preservation work of the techniques and traditions or processes that were in use when the building or structure was made and subsequently maintained through its life, must be juxtaposed with the preservation of the historic building itself. This is not to say that we should disregard the historic material contained in the structure left to us. However, we do not see any contradiction between maintaining the authenticity of an historic building and protecting the integrity of its fabric and design by using traditional materials and traditional craft techniques. The 'authenticity of processes' as a fundamental criterion for evaluating the genuineness of cultural properties, was proposed at the 1994 Bergen meeting on authenticity to replace the category of 'workmanship' in the Operational Guidelines of the UNESCO World Heritage Convention. We hope this concept will inspire conservation specialists, including craftsmen, to view historic timber structures not as static relics of the past but as a source of inspiration for keeping ancient traditions alive.

2.2 The principle of minimum intervention and maximum retention of materials

The major objective of current preservation theory and practice is to retain as much as possible of the existing materials of the historic building – both the original materials and those which have been added throughout history. The historic building should, if structurally and functionally possible, be preserved as it has been handed down to us through history. The identity and the genuineness or authenticity of the building is related to the substance acquired through its history. This theory was explicitly formulated by Alois Riegl in 1903 in his paper *Der moderne Denkmalkultus – sein Wesen und seine Entstehung* (The Modern Cult of Monuments – its Character and its Origin). Riegl's introduction of the concept of 'age value' (*Alterswert*) implies that we have to assume that everything which history has changed is irreversible and as such has become part of the historic building (Neuwirth, 1987; Petzet, 1995).

The aesthetic value of the historic building is, according to this theory, intimately linked to its value as an historical document. Further, the beauty of the building is not only related to its form but also to the weather-worn look – the 'patina' – of its materials. Only by retaining its old materials does the building appeal to us emotionally as an historic building. Both the artistic and historic value of the building are related to its authenticity in substance. This implies that in preservation work, as

Figure 2.1 Brookgate Hall, Plealey, is one of the oldest manor houses on the Shropshire border between England and Wales. The earliest part was built in 1350. In 1500 a wing was added. In 1612, part of the medieval structure was destroyed and a new parlour built. Photo before the restoration 1987–90 by the architect and owner, Graham Moss. The house had been empty for several years, the roofs were leaking and the house was in a bad state of repair

much of the old material as is technically feasible must be re-used.

In fact, this approach to the preservation of historic buildings goes back to the earliest days of modern preservation theory. As early as 1839, A. N. Didron, the director of the newly established French monument service, argued that minimal intervention is the best. In the Germanic countries, the same view was held by leading experts in the field. In 1856 August Reichensperger emphasised that the first and main rule in all restorations is to do as little as possible and as unnoticeably as possible (Jokilehto, 1986:

379). The argument was developed further by John Ruskin and the British Society for the Protection of Ancient Monuments in the latter part of the nineteenth century, and also emphasised by Max Dvorak in his *Katechismus der Denkmalpflege*. In fact, the mid-nineteenth century theorem 'Do as little as possible and as unnoticeably as possible' neatly sums up the overruling norm in the preservation philosophy of the late twentieth century. With this modest approach, the material authenticity of the historic building as it has been left to us by history is retained.

Figure 2.2   Brookgate Hall after restoration. Using the principle of minimum intervention, the architect conserved the timber structure and skilfully rebuilt the house to modern standards while retaining its historic atmosphere

2.3 Authenticity and material fetishism

The emphasis in current preservation theory and practice on the conservation of the historic fabric or substance may, in some cases, lead to a fetishism of material that is contrary to the broad main aim and perspective of preservation as this is outlined in the preamble to the Venice Charter:

> *Imbued with a message from the past, the historic monuments of generations of people remain to the present day as living witnesses of their age-old*

> *traditions. People are becoming more and more conscious of the unity of human values and regard ancient monuments as a common heritage. The common responsibility to safeguard them for future generations is recognised. It is our duty to hand them on in the full richness of their authenticity.*

The phrase 'in the full richness of their authenticity' implies that several issues are involved when we need to describe exactly what makes an historic building 'genuine' or 'authentic'. It is definitely not only substance which is essential. If we reduce our historic

Figure 2.3 Brookgate Hall after restoration. Detail of a gable showing replaced timber in the frame

buildings to substance, we may in fact jeopardise their values. According to Michael Petzet, we are not only dealing with the preservation of 'authentic documents' but rather of preserving historic buildings 'in the full richness of their authenticity'. He proposes that, based on the Venice Charter, it is possible to draw up a whole bundle of measures that can be used for an historic building, depending on the actual situation. Although he maintains conservation as the supreme preservation principle for the future as well, he asserts that alongside conservation, a whole range of intervention measures, such as restoration and renovation and even

reconstruction, must be accepted (Petzet, 1995: 93).

Petzet argues for a 'postmodern' pluralism where all possibilities must be considered in each different situation in preservation practice. He thinks that with the tremendously far-reaching preservation tasks on hand at the end of the twentieth century an approach to preservation ('a monument cult') that is fixated exclusively on 'historic fabric' simply no longer suffices (Petzet, 1995: 95).

2.4 *Firmitas – venustas – voluptas*

We agree with Michael Petzet that historic buildings are something more than just 'historical evidence', although the documentary value should not be neglected. We subscribe to Bernard Feilden's ideas when he proposes that we should have the same requirements for historic buildings as for contemporary buildings (Feilden, 1984). Thus, historic buildings must be:

1. durable and have the necessary strength and be able to withstand all types of loading, in short the structural integrity must be assured;
2. convenient to use, or functional;
3. pleasing to the eye, or delightful.

This is, in fact, the classical definition of architecture as proposed by Vitruvius in his treatise on architecture, *De architectura*, from the first century BC. The corresponding Vitruvian concepts are *firmitas*, *venustas* and *voluptas*. We believe that to take this complete view of historic buildings is in the spirit of the Venice Charter's advice to regard historic buildings 'in the full richness of their authenticity'.

To regard historic buildings as pure 'historical evidence' is not, in our view, to regard

Figure 2.4   Brookgate Hall after restoration. Interior of dining room

Figure 2.5   Well-maintained farm buildings in Val Badia, Italy

them in the full richness of their authenticity. Such a view limits the joy that historic buildings may transmit to future generations. According to the Swiss conservator Alfred Wyss, in our picture of how preservation should be carried out we have lost the aesthetic perspective. Some conservators warn of the danger that the cultural property may end up shining like a new building after restoration. They fear the perfect, the unnecessary interventions and the consequent loss of the opportunity to perceive authentic values and the possibility of re-restoration. Let us consider a country church, which has been carefully restored. Newly restored and painted, the church shines; it lives; it arouses the emotions. In this situation it cannot be right to diminish the joy of the congregation, who see the freshly renewed surfaces as an honour to God. This may be regarded as a living value of the historic building. Does this not to a large extent express a real continuity of heritage? Wyss warns us that we must not forget the pleasure of experiencing cultural properties. The maintenance of heritage must consider historical and technical analysis as well as including the aesthetic aspects of the building (Wyss, 1994).

On the other hand, we need to consider sustainable development, which encourages us to treat our resources, whether they are natural resources or other types, such as historic buildings, in such a way that they may be used by the present generation without compromising the chances of future generations of enjoying the same experiences as we have. Thus, we wish to conserve as much as possible of what has been handed down to us, but on the other hand we also have the liberty to interpret what we find, and, based on the historical and other knowledge sources available to us, hand down the historic building to future generations in the form that best satisfies the criteria of *firmitas, venustas* and *voluptas*, and consequently

displays the historic building in the full richness of its authenticity. Preservation may thus be seen as the way to allow the cultural property, through its materials and form, to speak in its own historical language. This implies that we are not only saving cultural properties for this generation but also so that the historic building can speak to future generations (Wyss, 1994: 126). In this perspective, the traditional knowledge of techniques of craftsmanship becomes an essential element of the communication process, both now and for the future.

2.5 Authenticity, timber structures and the replacement of members

The problem of replacement in wooden artefacts and the question of authenticity is age-old. It could be said that the discussion was introduced by Plutarch (*c.* 46–120 AD), a Greek biographer and author whose works strongly influenced the evolution of European literature from the sixteenth to the nineteenth century. Among his 227 works, the most important are the *Bioi paralleloi* (Parallel Lives), in which he recounts the noble deeds and characters of Greek and Roman soldiers, legislators, orators and statesmen, including the story of Theseus and the Minotaur. After killing the Minotaur, Theseus and his men returned to Athens in a wooden ship with thirty oars, which was preserved by the Athenians, who took away the old planks as they decayed, putting in new and stronger timber in their place. This ship became a standard example among the philosophers, with regard to the logical question of objects undergoing change (Lowenthal, 1992). Was it still the original ship? If not, when did it cease to be – when 50 per cent of the original material had been replaced; perhaps 51 per cent?

In this case, authenticity veers between shape and substance. These are the most

Figure 2.6   The Golden Hall (*Kondo*) of the Horyu-ji Buddhist temple in Nara, Japan – a World Heritage Site. Built in the late seventh century, this is the oldest timber structure in the world

obvious manifestations of the object's historical character. For example, people may perceive a building as old either because its materials appear old, due to wear and tear and to possible deterioration of its original qualities, or because the building may have a form based on a design which is not connected with contemporary aesthetic ideals. Object identity is still debated as a philosophical problem and the dilemma of Theseus' ship is analysed in new perspectives (Smart, 1972). The basic question, however, remains: can identity of form triumph over material authenticity?

Two examples from Japan illustrate the challenges we face in the discussion of the authenticity of timber structures where members have been replaced throughout

history (Larsen, 1994). The one is a Buddhist temple hall originally built in the seventh century, and the other, a three-storied pagoda built about the same time. These are timber structures more than 1300 years old. Both are included in the World Heritage List in 1993 within the site called *Buddhist Monuments in the Horyu-ji Area*.

The Golden Hall (*Kondo*) of the Buddhist temple Horyu-ji in Nara Prefecture, Japan, is considered to be the world's oldest wooden structure. The hall was erected in the latter part of the seventh century. During the Second World War, the roof structure and upper part of the hall were dismantled for repair. However, the dismantling was discontinued because the removal of the original interior wall paintings proved to be extremely

Figure 2.7 The Golden Hall of Horyu-ji. Members from the lower part of the temple hall, which were damaged by fire in 1949. These are conserved and exhibited inside a fire-proof warehouse adjacent to the original site

difficult. These were mural paintings on plastered wooden lattice (wattle and daub) in the bays between the pillars. Painters had started to make a replica but the work was not completed. Then, on 26 January 1949, disaster struck. The part of the Golden Hall which had not been dismantled, including the wall paintings, was severely damaged by fire. The wooden pillars, lintels and other members were charred to a depth of 3 centimetres. This meant that the damaged material could not be reused in a building that was still used for sacred ceremonies.

The members that were destroyed had been carefully measured and investigated before the fire, together with the ones that had been dismantled. It was decided that the hall should be reconstructed in its original form. The architectural concept of the original style was determined on the basis of the detailed investigations of the existing members and various historic documents. Accordingly, the lower part of the hall was constructed using new timber. The old, existing members, which had been removed during the dismantling, were used for the upper part. All new members were made of the same species of wood as used originally, Japanese cypress (*Chamaecyparis obtusa*). Furthermore, the carpenters dressed the new members using many of the ancient tools and techniques that had been used in the construction work in the seventh century.

Of the upper part of the restored hall standing in the Horyu-ji compound today, some members are original, dating from the

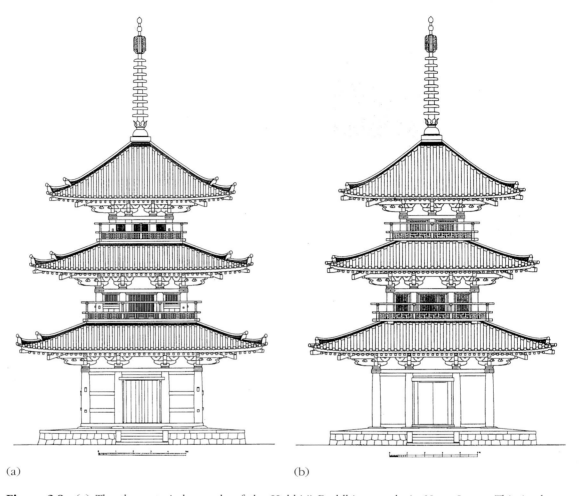

(a)   (b)

Figure 2.8   (a) The three-storied pagoda of the Hokki-ji Buddhist temple in Nara, Japan. This is also a World Heritage Site. Elevation before restoration in 1972–75. (b) Elevation after restoration. (Drawings from *Kokuho Hokkiji sanju-no-to shuri koji hokokusho*. Nara Prefecture Board of Education, 1975)

seventh century, but many have also been replaced, as the structure was completely dismantled, repaired and reassembled at the beginning of the twelfth century, in 1374 and in 1603. Probably no more than 15–20 per cent of the original materials exist in the present Horyu-ji *Kondo*.

Before the rebuilding of the present hall could start, the burnt lower part had to be removed. The charred surface of the members was extremely fragile and was consolidated using a synthetic resin; then the structure was carefully dismantled, and finally rebuilt within a fireproof concrete warehouse on the temple site. No new additions were made; the building stands inside the warehouse as a fragment, a ruin. Therefore, the world's oldest wooden building is in reality today two buildings. The burnt one is continuous in form and substance, although a fragment; the hall with its contemporary sacred functions is partially continuous in materials, and also only partially continuous in design, since it was restored to its original design from the seventh century. It must suffice to conclude here that this is a rare case, but still it can be regarded as an example of what may happen to timber structures, which burn readily. A fire may lead either to the complete loss of the materials, or they may be so badly damaged that it is not possible to reuse them in reconstruction.

The actual amount of original material, compared to material added through later repair, was carefully investigated by the outstanding Japanese architectural historian Masaru Sekino when the three-storied pagoda of the Buddhist temple Hokki-ji was repaired during 1972–5 (Sekino, 1978). The pagoda was erected around the same time as the Golden Hall of Horyu-ji, at the end of the seventh or the beginning of the eighth century. Consequently, this pagoda is also one of the oldest timber structures in the world. The main reason why it still exists, and contains a significant proportion of original members, is that the pagoda was repaired regularly – a process in which decayed members were replaced by new ones shaped in fresh timber, but the original members were kept if they were sound.

Documents confirm that the pagoda has been repaired seven times, of which three involved complete dismantling:

1. in the early twelfth century, the upper roof down to the bracket complex of the third storey was repaired;
2. the whole structure was completely dismantled and repaired in the thirteenth century;
3. in the fifteenth century the roofing was repaired;

4. in the seventeenth century the second complete dismantling was carried out. At that time several changes were made to the structure; for instance, the intercolumnar span of bays of the third storey was increased from two to three;
5. towards the end of the eighteenth century there was minor repair work;
6. major repairs were executed in 1897–8;
7. finally, between 1972 and 1975 the structure was completely dismantled for the third time, and during the reassembly the structure was restored to its presumed original state, in as far as this could be ascertained.

Sekino established the age of each member related to its position in the building. Naturally, the largest proportion of original members was located in the lower storey, and the amount decreased upwards. When considering the historical process of repair in this building, it is remarkable that as much as nearly half of the original members still exist. Thus, Sekino's investigation indicates that, throughout history, the repair of Buddhist temple buildings in Japan has been executed with respect for the preservation of existing, and in particular original, materials in the sense that the carpenters have reused as much as possible of the old material. The main thing to observe concerning these two timber structures from Japan is that replacement of members must be considered as an integral part of the history of timber structures. Continuous replacement is, in fact, the only way to preserve their authenticity as timber structures.

3

There is such great diversity

The essential message of the Nara Document on Authenticity is that the world's immense diversity of cultures and types of heritage should be respected:

> *The diversity of cultures and heritage in our world is an irreplaceable source of spiritual and intellectual richness for all humankind. The protection and enhancement of cultural and heritage diversity in our world should be actively promoted as an essential aspect of human development (Article 5).*

According to the Nara Document, this implies respect for other cultures and all aspects of their belief systems. Is it relevant then, one might wonder, within this extremely wide and tolerant perspective, to propose international preservation guidelines, such as the ICOMOS Wood Committee's Principles? What may be the common global factors in our efforts to protect and preserve timber structures made of wood?

We have found a common interest in trying to understand and interpret the working methods and techniques of those who designed and built historic buildings and those who have maintained them throughout history. The problem, however, is that we cannot fully understand historic timber structures without the help of skilled craftsmen. If craftsmen are to acquire and maintain relevant historic knowledge, they need practice in restoring and repairing actual buildings and structures. There is, therefore, a need to break away from the one-dimensional view of regarding preservation as concerning materials alone.

Although we hold this thinking to be universally applicable within the perspective of cultural and heritage diversity, we recognise that it may be a great challenge to implement a strategy of using traditional materials and techniques in repair work. In many places, the traditional techniques are outdated and it would take great effort to revitalise them. However, if we really want to understand our historic buildings, we need craftsmen skilled in ancient and traditional techniques.

As well as respecting the diversity of cultures and heritage, including building types, the Wood Committee's Principles address the diversity of wood species and their varying properties, and the vast array of organisms and other factors that may destroy our heritage of timber structures. As an approach to preservation, we propose that the use of traditional materials and techniques is an adequate response to these challenges. In fact, we believe they are more appropriate than the high-tech solutions and modern synthetic materials where long-term compatibility with ancient timber has not been documented.

3.1 Diversity of wood species and wood properties

Trees belong to two groups of seed plants: the gymnosperms and the angiosperms (Hoadley, 1990). The gymnosperms include all trees that yield the timber known commercially as 'softwoods'. Softwoods fall within four families of the order Coniferales, more commonly known as conifers, because they produce seed cones, pollen cones or both. They have needle-like (e.g., pine) or scale-like (e.g. cedar) leaves and are known as evergreens in that they retain their leaves for up to several years. There are, however, conifers that shed their leaves after the end of the growing-season, such as larch or baldcypress.

The angiosperms are separated into monocots and dicots. Monocots include bamboo and palms. The dicots include tree-sized plants known commercially as 'hardwoods', such as oak or teak. Hardwoods have leaves that are generally broad or blade-like. Most commercial species in the temperate zone are deciduous, that is, they shed their leaves during winter dormancy.

In total, 30 000 angiosperm tree species are known. Most of them grow in tropical forests. They far outnumber the gymnosperms, where only 520 tree species have been identified. The terms softwood and hardwood should not be taken as a measure of hardness, since some hardwoods, such as balsa, are much softer than many softwoods. The names of trees may also cause confusion. To give a particular wood its proper name, we should use its scientific (or Latin) name, as the common or trade names will often lead to confusion. Trade names are the names used by the timber industry. These may be different from the common names, used by most people when identifying trees. For example, in English, *Pinus sylvestris* may be called both 'European redwood' and 'Scots

Figure 3.1 Pine tree (*Pinus sylvestris*) from Sordal, southern Norway, approximately 600 years old

pine'. The scientific names are the only reliable ones for defining precisely a particular species. The first part of the scientific name indicates the genus (in the example above: *Pinus*) and the second part the species (above: *sylvestris*).

Although not all wood species are suitable for building purposes, timber is a building material which is generally available in most inhabited regions of the world. The type and quality of timber available to people has naturally depended on the prevailing climatic conditions and the condition of the soil, and

Figure 3.2 Oak (*Quercus robur*) in Spring Coppice, Powys, Wales

this has been reflected in the types of structure which have been erected, and in their durability. The types of timber in any one territorial zone have also varied greatly during the passage of time due to climatic changes, and this has led to successive changes in building forms (Davey, 1961: 32–33).

Architects and engineers responsible for the preservation of cultural heritage need to acquire a deep knowledge of the qualities of wood in order to understand and, when necessary, remedy the weaknesses of the historic buildings they are to protect. They must understand the specific qualities of the timbers used for construction work in their own countries, concerning aspects such as the macro- and microstructure of wood, wood anatomy and the chemical composition of wood. All these issues are important for the way wood behaves in actual use and how it may decay. Moreover, the architect and engineer should understand the physical and mechanical properties of wood relating to issues such as hygroscopicity (the relationship between wood and moisture), wood density and specific gravity, the thermal and acoustic properties of wood and the strength of wood, including the reasons for the directional variation in strength properties. For example, the extremely high tensile strength of clear wood, that is, wood without any defects, in the longitudinal direction, parallel to grain, is due to the structure of the cellulose molecule, the orientation of the microfibrils of the wood cell walls and cell orientation. This series of parallel longitudinal arrangements from the cellulose molecule to the longitudinal cells accounts for the high longitudinal strength of wood.

3.2 Diversity in decaying agents

Wood may decay due to attacks from fungi, wood-boring animals and bacteria. It may suffer damage through mechanical wear or be degraded or decomposed by chemicals. 'Weathering' leads to erosion of the wood surface. Finally, wood may degrade as a result of high temperatures or may be completely lost as a result of fire. The two main enemies, however, are fungi and wood-boring insects (Kirk and Cowling, 1984; Blanchette *et al.*, 1990; Weaver, 1993: 19–39).

Fungi are classified as plants in some classification systems but differ from all other plants in that they lack chlorophyll and the organised plant structures of stems, roots and leaves. Fungi 'feed' more like animals in that they require a ready source of nutrients which are broken down by enzymes produced in the 'body' of the fungus. The enzymes are released into the food source, which is gradually destroyed as the fungus grows within it. Fifty thousand species of fungi have been described, but it has been estimated that the total number may be as high as 100 000–250 000. Fungi are classified as parasites or saprophytes. Parasites obtain their food by infecting living organisms; saprophytes only attack dead organic matter, such as wood.

Animals, such as insects and marine borers, cause destruction to wood by burrowing into it either at the immature and adult stages or at the immature stage alone. In order to digest wood polysaccharides, insects and marine borers have the ability to reduce wood to finely ground digestible particles. Wood-decomposing insects and marine borers digest only the cellulose and hemicelluloses, either by enzymes or, as in the termites, by

Figure 3.3   Decayed timber in a nineteenth-century boathouse from Misvær, northern Norway

microbes in their gut. Certain wood-boring insects do not digest the structural polymers of wood. For example, in the lyctus beetle, wood passes through the gut, but only the easily digested non-structural materials, such as starch in parenchyma cells, are removed.

The animals which cause the most destruction to wood belong to the Insecta class, which is divided into 29 orders, of which five have members known to bore into wood. Some insects attack only hardwoods, some only softwoods, and some species attack both. Wood-destroying insects may be found in standing trees, in newly felled timber and in dried wood. During its life cycle, an insect

(a)

(b)

Figure 3.4   (a) Salone dei Cinquecento in the medieval Palazzo Vecchio in Florence, Italy. The Salone was rebuilt by Giorgio Vasari in the sixteenth century. (b) Detail of Vasari's elegant timber roof structure. All beams are planed. The iron reinforcement is part of the original structure

undergoes a complete metamorphosis, changing from egg to larva to pupa and finally to adult.

World-wide, there are about 2000 species of termites (Isoptera). Termites fall into six families, of which the two important wood-destroying families are the Rhinotermitidae ('subterranean' termites) and the Kalotermitidae ('dry-wood' termites). These termites extensively digest the polysaccharides in wood, while the lignin may be slightly altered (subterranean termites) or partly decomposed (dry-wood termites). As a result, termites destroy the structure of wood completely. Most termites live in the tropical and subtropical zones. However, their distribution also extends far into the temperate zone, both in the northern and southern hemispheres.

3.3 Diversity of timber structures

Wood, as one of the primary building materials, has been widely used in buildings all over the world as a structural, protective and decorative material (Mainstone, 1975; Chilton, 1995). In some regions, historic buildings are built completely of wood so that wood constitutes the structure as well as the architectural form. Timber structures also contribute significantly to the beauty and interest of stone and masonry architecture, such as the thirteenth-century timber domes of St Mark's in Venice and the many magnificent open timber roofs of English medieval architecture. However, since timbered roof structures often are hidden from view and are usually considered to belong more to the realm of engineering than to architecture, they have attracted less interest.

A particularly good example of this problem is the magnificent hall, known as the Salone dei Cinquecento, in the medieval Palazzo Vecchio in Florence. The Salone was rebuilt by Giorgio Vasari in the sixteenth century. Vasari raised the height of the room, remodelled it and decorated the room with wall paintings and a beautifully painted ceiling, some seventy years after the architect Simone Del Pollaiolo (il Cronaca) had built the room. Vasari's contribution as an architect and artist in this work has been acclaimed, but the timber roof, also designed by Vasari, is an excellent example of timber engineering. Of course, the decorated timbered ceiling could not exist without the superstructure, which carries this extremely heavy load. The roof timber structure ought to attract a level of interest which parallels that in the hall itself. Only by studying the elegant timber roof structure can we perceive the real value of Vasari's contribution, and this then changes our perception of the hall itself.

Through its use in joinery, wood also plays a central architectural role in countries or regions where the main structural material is stone or masonry, as for example in Nepalese historic buildings. External joinery includes architectural elements such as the balustrades of roof platforms and balconies, ornamental bargeboards, eaves, cornices, windows and window surrounds, doors and porches. Internal joinery includes wall panelling, shutters, skirting and doors together with architraves, panelled ceilings, floor-boards, staircases and stair balustrades. From this it follows that there is hardly any conservation project where the repair, conservation or restoration of wood is not involved.

In ancient times, the type of timber buildings was largely dependent on the available forest resources and the climatic and cultural conditions where they were built. In his study of European wood building traditions, the German architectural historian Hermann Phleps published an intriguing map of how the tradition found various expressions all over the continent (Phleps, 1942). Three types of timber structures are discernible: the

Figure 3.5 The Royal Palace in Patan, Nepal – a World Heritage Site

log structure, the post and beam structure and the timber-frame structure. It is remarkable to see from this map how the geographical distribution of the techniques is related to the available forest resources and the climatic conditions of the various regions. The timber-frame tradition dominates the central part of the European continent and England, and is related to the rich oak forests and a relatively mild climate. It extended northwards to the southern part of Sweden. Encircling the timber-framed buildings like a belt, we find the log-building tradition.

However, there are many regional and local variations within the main categories. This is one of the reasons why timber architecture is so fascinating. For example, within the log-building tradition, the shape of the

Figure 3.6 Map showing the distribution of the various types of timber structures in Europe. (Drawing from Phleps, 1942: 5)

logs varies, the techniques used to notch the intersecting logs in the corners may be more or less elaborate and the techniques used to adjust the logs to each other also show considerable variation.

In fact, the log building may be a good starting point to look at how ancient master-builders in various parts of the world used and benefited from the properties of wood in different ways. The log building consists of compact wooden walls with logs laid horizontally one upon another. Structural stability is provided by notching the logs at the corner intersections so that the wall

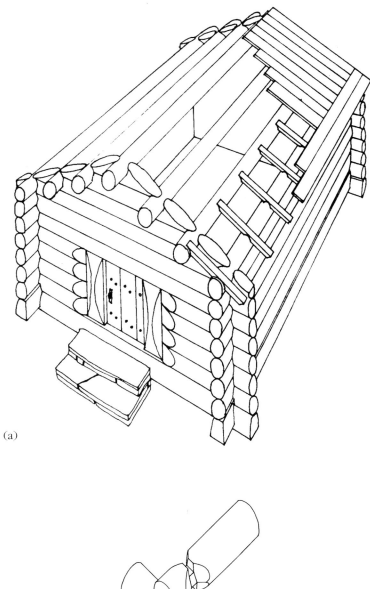

(a)

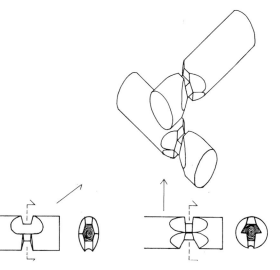

(b)

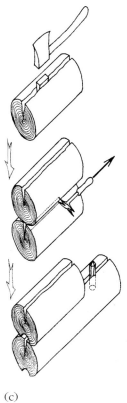

(c)

Figure 3.7   (a) Log construction; (b) typical corner notch; (c) conversion technique ensuring tight fit between the logs

Figure 3.8 A log structure from the Todai-ji Buddhist temple in Nara, Japan (Todai-ji Hokkedo Kyoko). This is the sutra repository, a storehouse for keeping the sacred books of Buddhism, built in the eighth century

planes interlock. The log buildings in the European region make use of one of wood's characteristic properties: its low heat conductivity, or, in other words, its high insulating value. Therefore, log buildings can be found in regions with relatively cold winters. In the same regions, there was also an abundance of straight-growing conifers.

This structural technique was used in the central European Alpine region, and extends eastwards encompassing several East European countries, such as Romania. It was widely used in Russia and dominant in Finland, Sweden and Norway for all types of buildings in the towns as well as in the countryside. The technique was used to build churches and mansions in the Nordic countries and in Russia, Poland, Romania and elsewhere. With the development of mecha-

nised sawing techniques in the sixteenth and seventeenth centuries, town houses, mansions and churches, built using the log-construction technique, were clapped with external boarding for protective as well as decorative reasons. European immigrants brought the log-building technique to North America in the eighteenth and nineteenth centuries.

The log-building construction technique is relatively rare when looked at from a global perspective. In addition to the areas of Europe mentioned above and in North America, log buildings are also found in some Asian countries, for example in Cambodia, the Yunnan province of China and in Japan. In these Asian countries, characterised by hot and humid climates, the use of the log-building technique was related to another of wood's favourable properties: its ability to exude or absorb moisture from the surrounding atmosphere until the moisture in the wood equals that in the atmosphere. In Japan, the log-building technique was used in the eighth and ninth centuries in particular, mainly for the construction of a particular type of temple building, the sutra repository, but also used for store-houses for valuable and fragile items. To preserve the sutra scrolls and other valuable items of textile, wood and paper, a stable internal climate in terms of relative humidity was important.

3.4 Timber structures and the world cultural heritage

In studies of world architecture, timber structures and wood as a building material have largely been ignored. There has been a widespread notion that timber structures belong to the vernacular tradition, and are therefore of lesser interest, while significant architectural monuments have been built in stone or brick. This notion is only partly true, as in many countries, like Japan and Norway, architectural monuments are made entirely of wood.

In this context, it is of interest to remember that even those architectural monuments made of stone were often modelled from wooden structures. Although disputed by some researchers, it is still widely held that the Greek Doric and Ionic orders have timber prototypes: timber forms were imitated in stone with remarkable exactness. We can observe a similar development of translation into stone of carpentry techniques in Indian architecture and in other parts of the Asian continent: Burmese monasteries were derived from timber prototypes and, in Cambodia, wooden buildings gave way to brick and stone imitations of timber prototypes.

In Scandinavia, and particularly in Norway, wood remained the most important building material until the beginning of the twentieth century. Thus the situation was the opposite: from the Middle Ages onwards, architectural forms in wood were often translations of European continental prototypes in stone or brick.

The most notable example of a country or region where timber structures have flourished as the ideal throughout history, is Japan. Here, timber structures completely dominated the building of all types of structures: castles, temples and domestic residences. As a result, Japan today has the world's richest heritage of timber structures, including the oldest and the largest historic timber structures in the world. In other Asian countries, such as Thailand, timber structures are important as part of the country's cultural heritage, but are not regarded with the same national or international interest as Thailand's magnificent monuments and archaeological sites composed of brick.

In spite of the importance of wood in history, and the fact that timber structures are important as cultural property all over the world, it is remarkable that so few timber structures have been recognised as World Heritage. Of the 112 countries which have sites inscribed on UNESCO's World Heritage List, only a very few have sites made exclusively of wood. These include sites such as Lunenburg old town in Canada, the Imperial Palace in Beijing in China, Petäjävesi old church in Finland, Buddhist monuments in the Horyu-ji area in Nara in Japan, the Ch'angdokkung palace complex in the Republic of Korea, the town of Luang Prabang in Laos, Urnes stave church in Norway, the old church complex of Kizhi Pogost in the Russian Federation, the church village of Gammelstad in Luleå in Sweden and the complex of Hué monuments in Vietnam. These sites with wooden buildings represent only a small fraction of the 418 cultural sites that were inscribed on the World Heritage List as of December 1997.

Figure 3.9 The hall of the Wat Phan Tao Buddhist temple in Chang Mai, Thailand

3.5 Diversity in wood detailing and woodwork joints

Throughout history, wooden buildings have been constructed in such a way that they did not carry the seeds of their own decline. If the carpenters of old had not been such excellent designers with a deep understanding of the uses and limitations of wood, there would not be anything left today which we could call an historic wooden house or timber structure. The most important consideration was to keep water away from the walls by using projecting eaves and by detailing all elements so that water could not accumulate.

We can see an extremely inventive approach in the sill beams of the medieval Norwegian stave churches which reflects the builders' deep understanding of what is required to make a timber building last. We believe the medieval Norwegian master-builders' solution in this case may illustrate an approach to the construction of timber structures which is universal in the sense that all master-builders knew that wood must be

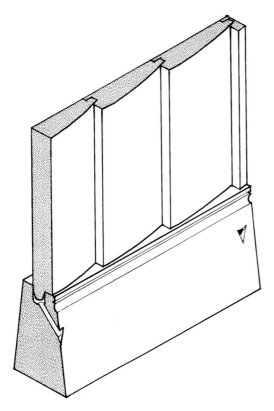

Figure 3.10 Lower section of outer wall, Kaupanger stave church, Sognefjord, Norway. The mortise in the bottom sill is made deeper to allow for possible water seepage. The water drains through angled holes in the sill

kept dry if it were to last. So here it is perhaps more a question of universality than diversity.

Another aspect of wood detailing is the woodwork joint, which is the junction of two or more members. Structurally, the greatest drawback of timber is the difficulty of making joints capable of transmitting and developing the tensile strength of the fibres; the transmission of compression is much easier. Considerable ingenuity has been devoted in the past to devising intricate ways of fitting members together to resist pulling apart from almost any direction. Perhaps woodwork joints show how carpenters could best demonstrate their understanding of structural

requirements as well as their most elevated, delicate techniques of craftsmanship. If we take a global look at woodwork joints, we will again observe universal elements, but perhaps to a larger extent, diversity in solutions. Some relatively complex lengthening joints that seem to be universal are, for example, the edge-halved scarf with square vertical bridled undercut and tabled abutments and folding wedges, and the stop-played scarf with vertical bridled undercut and tabled abutments and with folding wedges.

Many cultures exemplify the great diversity and elegance in architectural woodwork joints: for example, English medieval carpentry (Hewett, 1969). However, we have chosen to take a closer look at the magnificent details of Japanese carpentry. A traditional Japanese wooden building resembles a construction kit. All members could be prefabricated and afterwards assembled during the erection of the building. In a large building the number of members can reach 10 000. Metal fasteners, such as nails or cramps, are only used to a limited extent to tie members together. One of the key characteristics of Japanese architecture is that members are shaped to fit one another using woodwork joints (Larsen, 1994).

Although woodwork joints are prominent in Japanese architecture, carpenters took great pride in making the joints invisible. Close inspection of buildings is necessary to discover joints, which are in many cases due to later repairs. One of the most frequently used repair methods is the replacement of the decayed lower part of pillars. From a structural point of view it is dangerous to splice a vertical member in a building. Structural engineers usually strongly advise against this, because a splicing joint in a vertical member cannot transmit stress evenly and may snap under even a small lateral force. Numerous repairs of pillars by underpinning in Japanese historic buildings, some made centuries ago, reveal

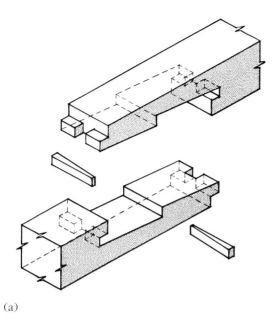

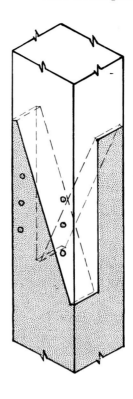

(a)

(b)

Figure 3.11 (a) Three complex lengthening joints; (b) scissor scarf joint for use on load-bearing members

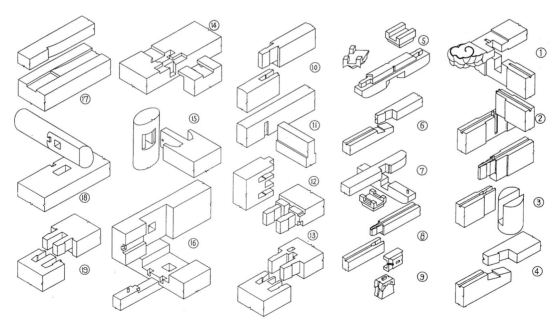

Figure 3.12 Joints used in the Nyoirindo hall of the Daigo-ji Buddhist temple in Kyoto, Japan. The hall was built in 1606. (Drawing from *Juyo bunkazai Daigoji nyoirindo shuri koji hokokusho.* Kyoto Prefecture Board of Education, 1964)

the skill of Japanese carpenters in woodwork jointing. They have devised several types of joints for this purpose, quite different and often simpler in design than the scissor scarf joint used to splice members in compression in English carpentry. What characterises the scissor scarf joint for use on fully load-bearing members, are the many planes of the joint providing greater resistance to movement in all directions than that provided by the simpler joint (Boutwood, 1991: 10).

Joints in Japanese woodworking are classified in two categories: lengthening joints and angle joints. Japanese experts have classified approximately fifty main types of lengthening joints and eighty main types of angle joints.

However, within these main types several subtle and intricate variations are found. Over the centuries the actual number of joints used by carpenters may be far in excess of 1000. The traditional techniques related to woodwork joints are today mainly used in preservation work when decayed parts of timbers are replaced by new, well-seasoned wood. This is an important aspect of the central idea in Japanese architectural preservation: on the one hand, jointing techniques are indispensable as a traditional preservation method, and on the other, the traditional techniques of woodwork joints are preserved through such work. These Japanese practices could well be emulated by others.

4

Desperate remedies: the benefits and drawbacks of modern technology

When interventions to conserve an historic timber structure become necessary due to decay and deterioration, the use of traditional materials and techniques should always be considered as the first option in the repair work. However, according to the Wood Committee's Principles, each intervention should be based on proper studies and assessments. Problems should be solved according to relevant conditions and needs with due respect for aesthetic and historical values and the physical integrity of the historic structure or site. Therefore, solutions other than those made in wood or other traditional materials and techniques may sometimes be more appropriate.

In particular, we may be tempted to consider the introduction of materials which differ from the original when we feel that the existing fabric has failed because of inherent defects in design or incorrect specification of materials, rather than from lack of maintenance (Brereton, 1995: 2). However, before such changes are made, we should consider whether, in fact, the building part may have completed its expected life. If we accept that we have to live with inadequate historic designs, this also entails accepting that problematic areas must be monitored more frequently, and that more frequent maintenance will be necessary.

As ideals, Article 5 of the Wood Committee's Principles advises that any proposed intervention should for preference:

(a) follow traditional means;
(b) be reversible, if technically possible; or
(c) at least not prejudice or impede future preservation work whenever this may become necessary;
(d) not hinder the possibility of later access to evidence incorporated in the structure.

In principle, the repair of timber structures may be approached in three ways. The first approach is to repair using available techniques and materials; for example, as in the repair of a medieval roof during the latter part of the nineteenth century when craftsmen used the techniques and materials of their own time. The twentieth century saw a huge development in the production of synthetic materials. We do not yet know their durability. If we insist that materials used in preservation work should be well tested, we will eventually have to turn to historical technology, and not rely on current technologies.

In Denmark, the civil engineering office of Eduard Troelsgård has introduced an approach to the repair of timber structures, where decayed wood is replaced by splicing

Figure 4.1   Hørsholm church outside Copenhagen, Denmark. Repair of rafters 1997. New and old timber is jointed and the joint reinforced with steel bolts and toothed-plate connectors

in new, seasoned wood and craftsmen work with contemporary tools and techniques. The company works very closely with carpenters from ordinary contractors, who are not specialists in conservation work. At the repair site, solutions are suggested to the carpenters while encouraging them to suggest alternatives. A typical repair joint in this case is a scarf joint reinforced with bolts and a toothed-plate connector. The aim of Troelsgård's company is to use solutions that are feasible within the framework of knowledge and experience of today's carpenters. They base their repairs on solutions that resemble old methods; decayed parts are replaced in a way familiar to today's carpenters while still rooted in tradition.

A second approach is to introduce new elements for the reinforcement of the old structure. In freely supported structures, like roofs, various reinforcement techniques using supports and additional elements have been widely used. In the case of open structures, like roof trusses, or framed structures, the criteria of Article 5 of the Wood Committee's Principles may, in many cases, best be fulfilled by reinforcing the weakened structural element using an additional structure, for example made of wood or steel. Replacement, on the other hand, whereby decayed wood is removed, is by nature a non-reversible intervention. However, replacement may satisfy criteria (b), (c) and (d). Replacement of ceiling joists is particularly difficult and expensive because of the risk of damage to floorboards above and the ceiling below. Repair should, where possible, leave the ceiling joists in place, while

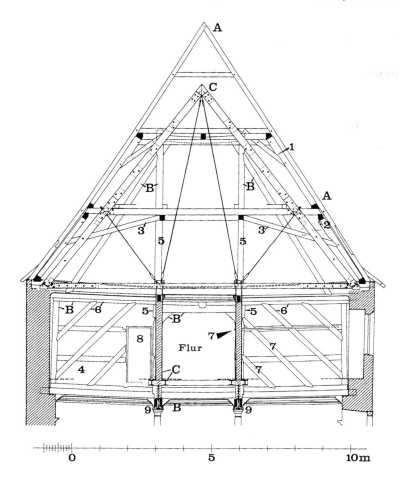

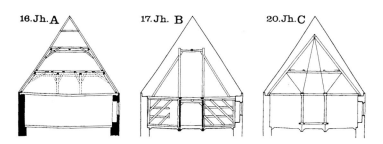

Figure 4.2 Grumbach castle, Rimpar, near Würzburg, Bavaria, Germany. The castle's medieval south wing was rebuilt in the early seventeenth century. During the rebuilding, the late Gothic and original roof trusses were kept largely intact, although today some parts are missing. The seventeenth-century rebuilding included strengthening the roof with an additional timber structure. At the beginning of the 1980s it had become necessary to strengthen the roof structure once again.

The situation was both unique and interesting: a preserved original roof structure, and an additional supporting structure that clearly demonstrated both the original building and the significant later rebuilding. After a careful survey and calculation of the existing structure, the Bavarian State Conservation Office decided that adding five identical wood and steel suspension structures in the length of the building would be sufficient to preserve the existing structure, as well as adding the necessary strength.

A, original sixteenth-century roof; B, seventeenth-century addition to the original roof structure; C, reinforcing structure from the 1980s; 1, 2 and 3, members from the original roof; 4, original wall paintings; 5, columns inserted during building phase B; 6 and 7, framed wall with braces built during phase B; 8, door inserted between building phases B and C; 9, longitudinal beams from building phase B. (Drawing from Mader, 1989: 50)

reinforcing them with timber or steel. Another option is to insert a new ceiling joist between the damaged ones (Gerner, 1994: 15–16).

The third approach is to re-build the structure, replacing damaged parts with new,

identical parts – that is, by copying. The result will depend on how well the carpenter can master the old tools and working methods or processes. In Archangel, Russia, the architect and carpenter Alexander Popov repairs historic timber structures in a very logical

Figure 4.3   Repair in timber by copying old members, Tokke, Norway

way: if a beam or log from the eighteenth century has to be replaced, he and his colleagues use the tools and techniques from that time; the same when a nineteenth-century beam or log has to be replaced. The carpenters have become extremely skilful in copying the craftsmanship techniques of ancient times by using the same methods and the same techniques. However, in both Russia and Scandinavia, particular carpentry techniques of the seventeenth, eighteenth and nineteenth centuries may no longer be so well known. Therefore, Popov and his carpenters have painstakingly studied old tools and the traces of tools in old buildings in order to understand the techniques and work processes (Ponnert and Sjömar, 1993: 35).

In the future we will need all three approaches or principles mentioned above. However, all preservation projects must be based on a deep understanding of historical structural techniques, and the knowledge of materials and old techniques of craftsmanship. Only when we have adequately mastered this do we have a real choice in selecting the right repair or restoration principle (Ponnert and Sjömar, 1993: 30).

4.1 Dismantling and rebuilding

Article 6 of the Wood Committee's Principles advocates minimum intervention in the fabric of an historic timber structure as an ideal. In certain circumstances, however, the

Principles allow that minimum intervention can mean that preservation and conservation may require the complete or partial dismantling and subsequent reassembly in order to allow for the repair of timber structures.

The aim should be, wherever possible, to stabilise the structure and replace or strengthen decayed members in situ. However, partial or complete dismantling and subsequent re-assembly or rebuilding may be allowed due to the character and particular requirements of timber structures, as well as relevant traditions. The question of repair through dismantling is quite controversial. In England, some experts call dismantling a crime or abuse of historic timber-framed buildings (Boutwood, 1992). Others allow partial dismantling and rebuilding if distortion of the timber frame or weakening of the structure is particularly far-advanced (Brereton, 1995: 13–14). When repair through dismantling of timber-framed buildings has been done by acknowledged English experts, like Fred Charles, it has been as a last resort to prevent the complete destruction of an historic building (Charles, 1984, 1992).

In Norway, the Directorate for Cultural Heritage has found that, with the exception of the sill beam and the upper log, the walls of medieval log buildings have generally not been repaired since they were built. Dismantling has no tradition as part of the repair process here: when the sill beam needed to be replaced, the carpenters jacked up the building. Today, when it is necessary to repair a log in the middle of the wall, small hydraulic jacks are used to force two logs apart in order to give the carpenter access to repair the decayed part, or to replace the log. This method works due to the flexibility of the structure and the nature of the corner joints, which give a log building its rigidity. However, the dismantling of log buildings is well known in Norway throughout history, because farm buildings were often moved from one site to another; in such cases dismantling was a convenient method. Farmers' daughters were often given one or more of the farm buildings as a dowry, in order to enable them to set up their own farms. The buildings would be dismantled and re-erected on a new site.

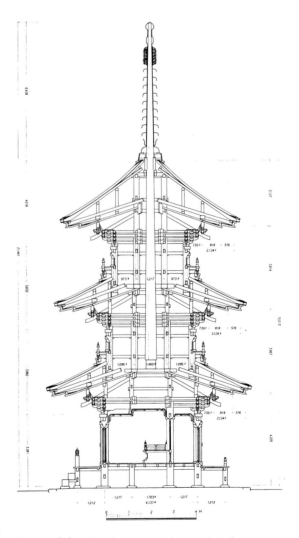

Figure 4.4 The three-storied pagoda of the Oyama-dera Buddhist temple in Ibaraki, Japan. The pagoda was completed in 1465. Cross-section. (Drawing from *Juyo bunkazai Oymadera sanju-no-to hozon shuri koji hokokusho*. Japanese Association for Conservation of Architectural Monuments/Agency for Cultural Affairs, 1991)

Figure 4.5   The central pillar of the three-storied Oyama-dera pagoda during preservation work in 1989. All members of the pagoda have been dismantled except the central pillar, which is suspended from the scaffolding

Japanese building traditions represent a special case in relation to dismantling and rebuilding as part of architectural preservation (Larsen, 1994: 68–81). Documentary evidence shows that since the ninth century the repair of timber structures has included dismantling and rebuilding at regular inter-vals. Based on experience, the preservation experts in Japan know with reasonable accuracy the durability of wood in the different parts of an historic timber structure, the durability of roofing, and of other materials – and consequently when repair is necessary. This knowledge is based on Japan's

(a)

Figure 4.6 (a) Oyama-dera three-storied pagoda. New bracket arms were inserted during the repair in 1989; (b) repair of the lower part of one of the four main pillars by splicing in new timber

(b)

immensely rich collection of extant historic records. The Japanese distinguish between five categories of periodical intervention in traditional timber structures, of which the two that are called 'major repairs' include complete or partial dismantling.

Every 300 to 400 years it is necessary to dismantle timber structures completely, member by member, down to the foundation stones in order to repair lower part of pillars, walls, etc. Furthermore, because the members are interlocked, it is impossible to remove them from the structure for repair unless the structure is dismantled. For instance, a bracket arm cannot be repaired before the bearing blocks above it are removed; because the bearing blocks are carrying the roof, the roof must be dismantled first. Moreover, complete dismantling is necessary at regular intervals because the timber structure itself fails due to loosening of the joints, or when partial sinking of pillar

stones and decay and warping of members occur. These defects cause the structure to incline. If the incline reaches three degrees, complete dismantling is of the utmost urgency.

'Half-dismantling' is carried out every 150 to 200 years. The major structural framework below the roof structure is kept intact. Other parts, such as roofing, roof structure, eaves bracketing and part of the walls are dismantled. Deteriorated parts are repaired and the building is then reassembled. If required, the structural framework is lifted and foundation stones are adjusted. Sinking of the long projecting eaves and decay of members in the upper part of the structure make dismantling of the roof necessary.

In addition, partial repair must be carried out in the intervals between the two major repairs (complete and half-dismantling). Some of the most deteriorated parts of the structure, for instance the eaves, clay walls,

(a)

(b)

Figure 4.7 (a) Oyama-dera three-storied pagoda (top part of the pagoda). Repair by jointing new, well-seasoned timber to the existing member; (b) the members before reassembly. The joint used in this case is an edge-halved scarf, with butts lipped and bridled

floor joists or verandas, are partially dismantled and members are repaired. Partial repair often also includes essential repair following typhoons and other disasters. Furthermore, between the major repairs, historic timber structures are re-painted and re-coated with *urushi* lacquer at regular intervals. Roofing has a relatively short life span in Japan; for example, cypress bark shingles last forty to fifty years and cedar shingles twenty to thirty years. Generally, it is necessary to renew the roofing completely. Again, this is always carried out using traditional techniques.

4.2 Replacement and reinforcement using wood

Article 9 of the Wood Committee's Principles recommends as the first option the use of timber and traditional carpentry techniques in repair work wherever possible. The Wood Committee's recommendation that repairs should be made using carpentry methods is a widely held view. For example, Christopher Brereton, in his handbook published by English Heritage, recommends that repairs to structural timbers should be carried out in timber using traditional carpentry methods, retaining all sound existing material, and replacing only what is necessary in order to restore structural integrity. Badly decayed or seriously split members or parts of members should be carefully cut away and new sections spliced in, using timber of the same species and scantling as the original (Brereton, 1995: 27). The use of repair joints puts heavy demands on the skills of the carpenters, as mentioned in the preceding chapter.

It is very important for the success of the repair work that architects, engineers and carpenters work together right from the start of the project, during the inspection, to determine what should be done to the building or

Figure 4.9 Old windows stored at the workshop of the Bavarian State Conservation Office at Thierhaupten, Bavaria, Germany

Figure 4.8 New members or parts of members should have the date of the repair inscribed on them so that they can be identified later. Here is an example from Japan where the date of the repair is burnt into the wood. The characters mean *Heisei gannen go boshu*, that is: this piece of timber was put into the structure in 1989, the first year of the Heisei era

structure. Thus, it is possible to save time since the carpenter may be able to dismiss repair proposals that are not practicable. Japanese conservation architects, together with the carpenters, sketch out on paper and also on the timbers in situ, the repair joints which should be used in various cases throughout the repair project.

Finally, concerning replacement timbers, the Wood Committee's Principles recommend that new members or parts of members should have the date of the repair discreetly carved, or burnt into the wood or be dated by other methods, so that they can be identified later. Such information can be invaluable both to historians and to those working on the repair of the building in the future (Boutwood, 1991: 12).

During repair work, it may be necessary to remove timbers from the building or structure which are significant for the understanding of its history. In such cases the Wood Committee's Principles recommend that removed members and other components of the historic structure should be catalogued, and characteristic samples kept in permanent storage as part of the documentation.

4.3 Replacement using epoxies

Epoxies or epoxy resins belong to a group of synthetic chemicals called polyethers. Epoxy resins were commercially introduced in 1946 under the trademark Araldite by a Swiss chemical company. Since the 1960s, epoxies have been used extensively in Europe, North America and Japan to repair decayed timber in historic buildings. According to Article 10 of the Venice Charter, new methods and techniques should have been proved by experience before being used to repair cultural properties. Epoxy mortars have now been used for nearly forty years. The question is, is this a sufficient length of time? The answer probably depends upon the perspective one takes. When dealing with cultural properties which are 100 years old, forty years may certainly seem like a sufficient period. When the cultural properties are closer to 1000 years old or more, forty years may seem insignificant. We like to think that when we are dealing with cultural properties that may have existed for centuries, our interventions should also have a durability perspective of a similar span.

The use of resins in timber repair should be considered with great care and normally only where carpentry methods are impracticable. The major structural uses of the epoxy resins are in the in situ repair of timber beam ends, the grouting and filling of timber sections excavated by fungal and insect attack and the in situ strengthening of floor-beams. Epoxies are also used as adhesives in structural and other repairs in timber structures. Epoxy mortars have largely been used to repair timber beam ends. Combined with the use of stainless steel or polyester rods, the epoxy mortars have sufficient strength to perform the same role as the original timber. Repairs can be carried out without disturbing other parts of the building (Ashurst and Ashurst, 1988: 19). However, epoxies should not be used in connection with joints as this will prevent the structure from adjusting itself through the free movement of the joints in response to stresses (Boutwood, 1991: 5; Brereton, 1995: 31).

Apart from the companies who make their living by carrying out epoxy repairs, most experts now agree that epoxies should not be used for external repairs. The reason is that we have no control over what may happen in the interface between the old, sound wood and the plastic material. Firstly, it is quite likely that water may penetrate behind the resin, followed by an accelerated rate of decay. Secondly, in cases where resins seal the wood externally, natural vapour pressure in the wall shifts the damp to the internal surfaces of the resin reinforcements, leading to condensation and possible decay. In addition, one should also consider the general problem that because of differences in their ways of action, new stronger structures cause damage to the weaker original (e.g. reinforced concrete cast together with historic masonry; wood built in with plastic, etc.). Damage always occurs at the interface between various materials and it is the weaker part that will be damaged first. In Scandinavian preservation work, experts have learnt that rarely it pays to break away from the original techniques and materials without there being serious consequences in the form of accelerated deterioration (Holmström, 1993: 12–13). Moreover, the repair and consolidation of decayed wood with epoxy resins are definitively irreversible.

When the original materials have been converted to plastic, are they still 'the original materials'? To reinforce a beam, the plastic part must be anchored to the fresh wood by reinforcing fibreglass rods or steel plates. In other words, holes must be drilled or a groove cut in the fresh timber to accommodate the reinforcement, thus destroying original material. Would it not be better to splice in new wood, as this would leave the original material untouched? In fact, this may allow even more original material to be preserved, as then we may avoid drilling holes or cutting grooves for the reinforcing elements.

The real problem here is the decay of beam ends at the point where they rest in brick or stone walls. Builders have probably always been aware of this and opted for solutions to avoid the problem. An interesting discovery was made in connection with the reconstruction of St Catherine's church in Stockholm, Sweden, after a fire in 1990. The restoration architect, Professor Ove Hidemark, discovered that during the eighteenth century, when St Catherine's church was built, carpenters used to wrap the beam ends that were inserted into brickwork with birch bark (Berggren, 1994; Hidemark, 1996). This natural material is excellent in its capacity to keep water away from timber, and may thus prolong the life of wood inserted into brickwork by centuries. It would be interesting to know whether similar approaches have been tried in other countries. Traditional protective methods such as the use of birch bark on beam ends embedded in masonry do not solve the problem of decayed beam ends but they certainly help us to prolong the life of the new wood used to replace the decayed part.

4.4 Steel reinforcement

Reinforcement of timber structures using iron members goes back at least as far as the Renaissance in Europe, although forged nails were used to connect lighter members as early as the Middle Ages. For instance, iron straps were used in bridge designs, like those of Palladio of 1570 (Mainstone, 1975: 154). When engineered timber designs developed during the second half of the eighteenth century onwards, the use of timber structures reinforced with iron became more common and sophisticated. Today, there is a wide variety of steel and stainless steel mechanical fasteners and connectors, such as nails, staples, screws, bolts, nail-plates, beam and joist hangers and timber connectors of various designs, as well as custom-made welded assemblies, for joining members.

The use of steel in the repair and reinforcement of historic timber structures also has a long history, dating back to the nineteenth century. Thus, technical solutions from that

time which have, in accordance with Article 10 of the Venice Charter, been proved by experience, may also be used today without problems. However, not all technical solutions involving steel have proven themselves sufficiently, and great care should also be taken when using steel repairs and reinforcements. As a general principle, it is always better to use new timber rather than steel when repairing timber structures (Boutwood, 1991:6). Under certain climatic conditions there may be problems in using steel in direct contact with wood because condensation on steel plates leads to accumulation of humidity which causes wood to decay. Moreover, corroded steel causes discoloration of the wood. We are therefore somewhat suspicious of the idea that steel reinforcements should be concealed when used in connection with exposed timbers (Ashurst and Ashurst, 1988: 17). Because of the danger of condensation on steel, most experts agree that steel reinforcements should always be visible and open to inspection (Charles, 1992).

Steel has frequently been used in the repair of beams which may have decayed due to rot or insect infestation or fractured because of over-loading. Timber beams always fracture first on the under-side because it is the tensile portion of the beam which is weakest. A number of technical solutions may be used to repair timber beams that are decayed, have fractured or need strengthening for other reasons, and where floorboards or ceilings beneath may be particularly valuable and replacement or repair would disrupt the construction (Macgregor, 1991). However, strengthening beams or joists with steel is an intervention that also has drawbacks. While it will take several hours before a timber beam is charred and completely destroyed by fire, floors that have been strengthened by the use of steel elements will be more vulnerable to failure. Therefore, if floors have been strengthened by steel, additional fire

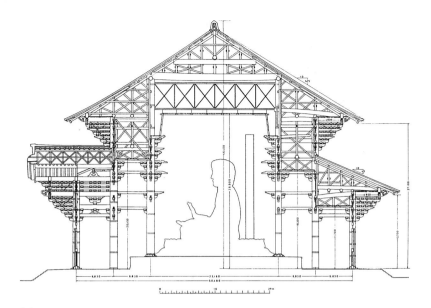

(a)

Figure 4.10 (a) The Great Buddha Hall (*Daibutsuden*) of the Todai-ji temple, Nara, Japan. Section after the restoration of 1903–13 when steel girders were added to reinforce the structure. (b) Steel reinforcement of the timber frame and reinforcement of a bracket complex with flat steel bars done during the restoration of the hall 1903–13. (Drawings from *Kokuho Todaiji kondo (Daibutsuden) shuri koji hokokusho*. Nara Prefecture Board of Education, 1980)

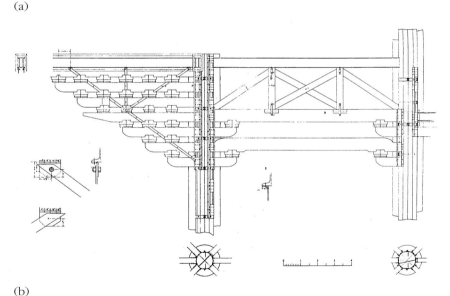

(b)

4.4.1 Case study: steel reinforcement in Japan

The Japanese have a long and relatively successful history of the use of iron or steel reinforcement of timber structures dating back to the latter half of the eighteenth century. In particular, the Great Buddha Hall (*Daibutsuden*) of the Buddhist temple Todai-ji, the world's largest historic timber structure, was given an overall steel reinforcement during repairs in 1903–13. A double steel roof truss was inserted to support the frame of the

protection of the building or structure may be required.

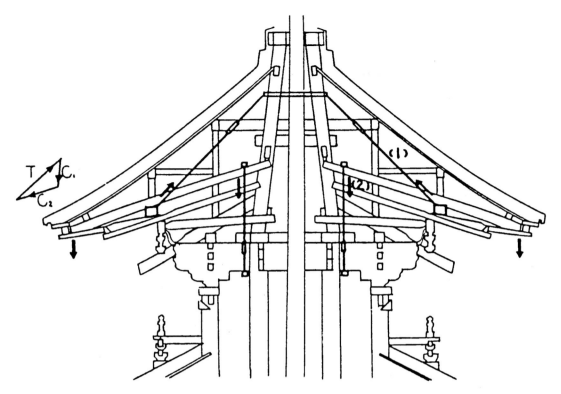

Figure 4.11 The three-storied pagoda of the Kiyomizu-dera Buddhist temple in Kyoto, Japan, built in the early seventeenth century. Cross-section of the upper roof. During the repair, completed in 1986, turnbuckles were introduced to reinforce the roof structures carrying the load of the projecting eaves. (Drawing from *Juyo bunkazai Kiyomizudera sanju-no-to shuri koji hokokusho*. Kyoto Prefecture Board of Education, 1986)

large roof, all bracket complexes were reinforced with flat steel bars, rafters and extended beams were reinforced with thick steel plates, and the central part of pillars was reinforced with steel channels. The reinforcement has functioned remarkably well, and no deformation of the main structure can be observed today, after nearly one hundred years (Kaneta, 1978: 96–97). Japanese experts are, however, fully aware of the problems connected with the use of steel in combination with wood and aim to find structural solutions which avoid them (Kaneta, 1978: 124).

Since the 1980s, structural reinforcement of roofs with turnbuckles has been used to great advantage (Larsen, 1994: 96–99). A traditional Japanese timber structure with deep overhanging eaves carries the seed of its own destruction, because the eaves tend to sink. The degree and speed of sinking is dependent on the size of the building, but even comparatively small roofs, as in pagodas, tend to sink. If the sinking is uneven, the eaves line becomes wavy and the building becomes unsightly. As the gently curved eaves line is such a prominent feature in Japanese traditional architecture, such sinking must be termed destructive. To remedy this defect, the roof construction must be dismantled and reassembled in order to readjust the eaves line to its original position. When this is

Figure 4.12   Pieced-in repair of a door, Mosjøen, Norway

done, turnbuckles and other steel reinforcement are introduced to prolong the period where the roof line is kept in the original position.

4.5 Preserving and repairing the whole building

Article 7 of the Wood Committee's Principles recommends where intervention is necessary, the historic structure should be considered as a whole. All material, including structural members, in-fill panels, weather-boarding, roofs, floors and joinery should be given equal attention. In principle, as much as possible of the existing material should be retained. The preservation should also include surface finishes such as plaster, paint, coating, wallpaper, etc. If it is necessary to renew or replace surface finishes, the original materials, techniques and textures should be duplicated as far as possible. It is recognised that the wall cladding, infill, etc. are of historical and aesthetic value, and they may also be important as structural elements (Boutwood, 1991: 5).

Several of the principles used in repairing structural timbers also apply to the repair of joinery. Attacks by fungi and insects are the main agents of decay here as well (Brereton, 1995: 54). Again, only what is strictly necessary should be replaced. The carpenter should use timber of matching species and type of grain, and the wood must be well seasoned. Conservative pieced-in repair should be used to replace decayed parts with the aim of keeping as much as possible of the original material (Brereton, 1995: 54–56).

5

The two sides of the coin: preservation of structures and preservation of techniques of craftsmanship

The repeated replacement of destroyed or decayed parts and repair by craftsmen is a part of the traditional maintenance of an historic timber structure and must be accepted as a valid aspect of the cultural and historical value of the structure. It follows from this that knowledge of the intangible traditional techniques of craftsmanship is itself as worthy of preservation as the material or tangible resources.

Although this way of thinking is shared by many timber structure preservation specialists all over the world, it is also controversial in the sense that some may see it as a violation of the principle that regards the conservation of substance or historic material as the sole essential aspect of preservation. Some outstanding experts warn against what they regard as an increasingly widespread ideology, such as in the Wood Committee's Principles, where craft techniques are proposed as the preferred approach to repair. It is not the task of the preservationist, in the opinion of these experts, to pay homage to techniques of craftsmanship, but to preserve the historical findings with the most appropriate technological means (Mader, 1991: 68). It may well be that high-tech modern solutions may be appropriate in many cases

Figure 5.1 Tools used by carpenters in the repair of the three-storied Oyama-dera pagoda, Japan in 1989: adze and axe; two kinds of chisels – used by pushing (*left*), or by striking (*tool box in centre*); planes – *left*, a common plane; *centre*, rebate planes; *right*, moulding planes

Figure 5.2   Axes used by Norwegian carpenters in the repair programme for medieval timber structures, 1991–96

where buildings or structures made from other materials are concerned. However, the situation is different for timber structures, due to wood's propensity to decay when compared with stone or brick, and the necessity of replacing members at intervals. The recommendation of Article 5 of the Wood Committee's Principles of using traditional craft techniques for preference, is based on the experiences of countries with long traditions of building in wood, such as England, Finland, Japan and Norway. In fact, Japanese practices in this field could with benefit be emulated by other nations.

The Japanese systematically promote the use of historic materials, techniques of craftsmanship and construction techniques in preservation work. Moreover, Japanese heritage legislation provides for the protection of historic techniques and recognises people and institutions who can transmit the knowledge of these techniques to future generations. The Japanese have come to recognise a mutually dependent relationship between the preservation of historic buildings and the preservation of historic techniques. As a consequence, the Japanese have taken a leading position in the world in the systematic study and use of historic materials and techniques in preservation work (Larsen, 1994).

5.1   Preservation of buildings and preservation of traditional techniques in Japan

The techniques used in erecting sophisticated Japanese historic buildings are outdated

Figure 5.3 Tsunekazu Nishioka planing with the spear-shaped plane (*yari-ganna*). The Yakushi-ji Buddhist temple in Nara, Japan, 1987

specifications. Architectural historians play an important part in architectural preservation, to a larger extent than in other countries. Japanese experts have realised the importance of architectural preservation work and have used it as a primary source of obtaining new information about architectural development in their country.

A new approach to the use of traditional but outdated tools and techniques in repair work was initiated during the repair of the buildings of the temple of Horyu-ji between 1935 and 1955, including the reinstatement of the Main Hall after the fire in 1949 (Larsen, 1994: 82–86). The architect in charge of the project was the eminent architectural historian Kiyoshi Asano, and the master-carpenter was Tsunekazu Nishioka. The Japanese Agency for Cultural Affairs has recognised Tsunekazu Nishioka as a 'Holder of Traditional Conservation Techniques' for his competence in traditional carpentry.

Asano and Nishioka carefully studied both the surface of the timbers and old documents to decide what kinds of tools the carpenters had used in the seventh and eighth centuries, and which postures the carpenters assumed when handling the tools while dressing the timber. Their studies prompted a revival of historic tools that were no longer in use, particularly the spear-shaped plane (*yari-ganna*). Their investigations showed that in the case of pillars, the timber had first been hewn with an adze, and then the surface had been finished with the spear-shaped plane. The *yari-ganna* leaves a quite distinct surface pattern, resembling a bamboo leaf. According to Nishioka, a wooden surface finished with a *yari-ganna* stays smoother for a longer period than surfaces finished with ordinary planes. The cut is so clean along the cell walls of the wood that it prevents penetration of water and makes the wood more resistant to attack by fungi (Brown, 1989: 76). Thus, the seventh-century Japanese carpenters' skill

today, but are nevertheless used in architectural preservation work. The Japanese recognise that traditional techniques are necessary in order to preserve historic structures, and conversely, traditional techniques are being preserved through actual preservation work. The mutually dependent relationship between the preservation of buildings and the preservation of traditional techniques is the central tenet of contemporary architectural preservation philosophy in Japan. Japanese architects and carpenters engaged in architectural preservation base their work upon a thorough knowledge of traditional materials, building technology and design

Figure 5.4   Surface of a beam of Japanese cypress (*Chamaecyparis obtusa*) prepared using the *yari-ganna*

with the *yari-ganna* when working with top-quality Japanese cypress (*Chamaecyparis obtusa*) goes a long way towards explaining why a large percentage of original timbers can still be found in preserved buildings from the seventh and eighth centuries.

Interestingly, a similar discovery was made in Norway in the 1990s, when carpenters started to study the surface of medieval timber structures in order to understand what kind of tools the medieval carpenters had used. They found traces of tools which they were certain must have been caused by the use of a spokeshave. The mark left by the medieval Norwegian spokeshave was quite similar to that left by the Japanese *yari-ganna*, and the surface of the timber where the cut had been made also felt quite similar, being very soft to the touch. We suggest that

the spokeshave also cut the wood fibres very gently, thus contributing to the preservation of the timber.

Returning to Japan, the method which Asano and Nishioka introduced through their work at Horyu-ji has since been faithfully adopted by Japanese conservation architects. If a member in a timber structure has to be replaced, they try to obtain the same species with the same grading and the same natural characteristics as was used originally. Further, the new member will be dressed with similar tools to those used by the original carpenters, and, where possible, the carpenters assume the same work postures when handling the tools in order to obtain a surface texture identical to the original. Japanese conservation architects claim that if this approach is used, the new member will fit better into the

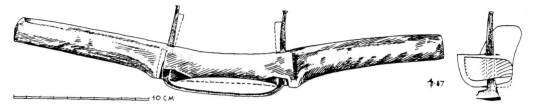

Figure 5.5   Spokeshave used in Norwegian carpentry since medieval times. (Drawing from Berg, 1989: 23)

Figure 5.6   Carpenter planing a log with a spokeshave

techniques been emphasised to the same extent as in Japan. It is also unique in that traditional knowledge is protected through provisions in the preservation legislation.

5.2 Research on technology and history of materials

In order to understand the builders and carpenters of former times, to obtain knowledge about their tools, to identify regional and local schools, to discover, amongst other things, how innovations in building technology spread, we must be able to interpret the traces left by the tools of the ancient builders on the timbers of existing buildings. Investigation of building techniques and construction technology, craft techniques and the use of materials should, therefore, be an integral part of architectural preservation work when dealing with historic timber structures. In order to analyse historic craft techniques and building technology it is a prerequisite that craftsmen and building historians work together. Thus, the knowledge that has been carried by tradition will enter the realm of scientific knowledge, which is necessary if the traditions are to survive. It is the carpenters who have the key to a really deep understanding of the art of timber construction.

An example of this is the North European medieval carpentry technique known as *sprett-telgjing* in Norwegian, which was used

original structure, both technically and aesthetically. New timber that is used in repair work is always well seasoned.

Nowhere has the mutually dependent relationship between the preservation of buildings and the preservation of traditional

Figure 5.7 Boards inserted into the gallery wall of a Norwegian medieval timber structure during repair work. The boards have been planed using a spokeshave

Figure 5.8 Carpenter at the repair site of the three-storied pagoda of Oyama-dera, Ibaraki, Japan in 1989, planing. The long, perfect shaving is a trademark of the excellence of Japanese carpentry work. The carpenter is pulling the plane

Figure 5.9 A sill beam prepared using *sprett-telgjing*

to finish the surface of exposed timbers in log buildings (Ponnert and Sjömar, 1993: 27). In Scandinavia, until the mid-nineteenth century, the axe and the adze were the tools normally used to produce beams and boards. The term adze in Scandinavian carpentry denotes a broad-bladed axe, not – as in English – a tool with a thin arched blade at right angles to the shaft. However, the function is the same: a tool used for squaring logs, levelling horizontal surfaces, etc. The methods for using the adze and axe varied depending on date and location.

Sprett-telgjing is an extraordinary method used in Northern Europe, including Norway, Sweden and Northern Russia, to level timber surfaces. No examples of the *sprett-telgjing* technique later than the mid-fourteenth century have been found in either Sweden or Norway. In other words, the Black Death

represented a turning point in the use of the technique; the last examples are from the period 1350–70. The characteristics of the *sprett-telgjing* technique are evident from its name. The verb *sprette* means to bounce: to strike a surface and spring back or rebound. The verb *telgje* means to whittle (by adze). The adze rebounds after first having cut into the wood. Instead of making a cut where small chips stand out from the wood, like the cut which is the result of later techniques, the surface became extremely smooth and shell-like through *sprett-telgjing*. As with the Japanese spear-shaped plane, the *yari-ganna*, and the Norwegian medieval spoke-shave, mentioned above, the wood fibres were cut very delicately using the *sprett-telgjing* technique. This may well have contributed to the long life of the timber in Scandinavian medieval buildings.

The use of the *sprett-telgjing* technique in Nordic medieval carpentry has been observed in different building types and used for various elements: in the roof structure of early medieval churches, such as in the rafters and beams and in roof boards, and in early medieval farm buildings in parts such as the underside of floorboards, or in sill beams. Members of pine, spruce and oak have been treated using *sprett-telgjing*. No marked differences have been observed in the use of the technique over time and no marked local differences exist.

When carpenters in Norway and Sweden tried to revive the technique at the beginning of the 1990s, they were not able to reconstruct the old surfaces perfectly. They asked themselves whether the medieval carpenters had used a differently shaped axe-blade, whether the handle could have been longer or shorter, etc. Suddenly the period of Russian *glasnost* opened up the way for co-operation with Russian architectural conservators and craftsmen. Then Norwegian and Swedish carpenters discovered that the *sprett-telgjing* technique had been regularly used in Northern Russia right up until the end of the eighteenth century, and was still known by some carpenters. Scandinavian carpenters were therefore able to learn and revive this medieval carpentry technique.

According to oral tradition from Archangel, Russia, the master-carpenter would make an apprentice who had not managed to prepare a beam adequately with *sprett-telgjing* take off his trousers and use his bare backside to test the surface of the log. In this way they learned how such a prepared surface ought to feel. Whether the story is true or not, it serves to illustrate one of the objectives of the technique: to achieve an absolutely smooth surface where no chips stand out. *Sprett-telgjing* was a way to obtain a surface similar to, or perhaps even smoother than, a planed surface (Ponnert and Sjömar, 1993: 28).

5.3 The revival of traditional carpentry techniques and repair methods

When the traditions of carpentry techniques have been broken, how may we revive them if we think that the ideal in architectural preservation is to use such techniques in repair work? The solution is, as mentioned above, what happened in Japan when the temple of Horyu-ji was restored from 1935 onwards: to launch a project where architectural historians and carpenters work together in order to analyse and try to understand the traces of tools they find on the old timbers of historic buildings. In Scandinavia, the heritage preservation authorities made a similar realisation at the beginning of the 1990s. The Swedish National Board of Antiquities established a project to study the traditional uses of wood in construction (Ponnert and Sjömar, 1993: 34–35). In Norway the Directorate for Cultural Heritage established a programme to repair medieval timber structures in private ownership, which became known as the 'Medieval Programme' (Haslestad, 1991, 1993a, 1993b).

In 1990 the Directorate for Cultural Heritage in Norway had listed some 250 timber structures from the Middle Ages. Of these, there were the twenty-eight stave churches and the rest were mostly vernacular buildings belonging to private farms, and a few to local, regional and national museums. These were mostly log buildings representing various categories of farm buildings, such as houses, store-houses, barns etc. In 1990, the Directorate for Cultural Heritage proposed that the Ministry of Environment should make a five-year contribution to the preservation of the vernacular medieval timber structures with the intention of developing this programme into a model project for the repair and restoration of timber structures in general. According to Norwegian heritage

Figure 5.10   A repaired medieval timber building in Tokke, Norway. Only minor repairs have been made to the log structure. The roof boarding has been completely renewed

legislation, all buildings from the Middle Ages are automatically listed. As automatic listing places a heavy burden on the owners, the Ministry felt it had a duty to relieve them of some of this burden through a contribution towards the cost of the repair of medieval timber buildings in their custody.

In 1989, the first volume of a series of books on the preserved vernacular medieval buildings in Norway was published. The series is written by and based on the research of architect and grand old man of Norwegian architectural history, Arne Berg. In 1989 only about 200 buildings were known. In 1991 the number of vernacular medieval timber structures had increased to 225, and in 1996, when the 'Medieval Programme' was completed, the number had increased to 250. This discovery of buildings during the programme period can mainly be attributed to carpenters who had taken part in the programme in their own districts. As the carpenters became familiar with the various building and wood carving techniques from the Middle Ages,

they were able to recognise in their home villages medieval buildings that had previously been unknown to researchers.

At the start of the programme, some of the medieval buildings were in a good state of repair, while others were close to collapse and were in danger of being lost forever. The rate of deterioration had accelerated during the past thirty to forty years, particularly for agricultural buildings that were no longer used. The main purpose of the programme was to leave each building in a good state of repair, so that future maintenance could be dealt with by the owner without excessive costs. It was the aim of the programme that the buildings should be repaired so that they could act as examples for local preservation work. Therefore, the Directorate for Cultural Heritage decided to accept only traditional materials of the highest quality and to make no compromises concerning techniques.

An important part of the programme was to locate and activate those bearers of tradition who could contribute to the revitalisation of old, traditional crafts and techniques. Thus, through the project programme, experienced carpenters and other craftsmen acted as instructors both in theoretical and practical teaching programmes. However, the Directorate for Cultural Heritage also took into account the importance of local knowledge; thus, a craftsman who represented a specific local tradition did not teach for extended periods of time in another region, in order to prevent locally based building traditions being exported to other regions. The programme aimed to keep the traditional diversity of locally or regionally based technical solutions and carpentry techniques.

Craftsmen who took part in the programme were required to participate in a training course organised by the Directorate for Cultural Heritage. A building later in date than the actual medieval repair project, and often located near to the medieval timber structure, was chosen as the training area or object. The carpenters were compensated from the programme budget for the loss of income for the duration of the courses. The training courses for the carpenters lasted from two to six weeks. Some of the first carpenters who took part in the programme were gradually promoted to instructors. During the programme more than sixty carpenters were trained.

Participants in the training programme reached a level of competence which is in high demand in their localities, from museums, local and regional conservation officers and the Directorate for Cultural Heritage. Many of the carpenters who took part in the programme were farmers as well as craftsmen. This double income is often necessary in Norway in order to enable people to make a living in rural areas. Thus, the competence these people acquired through the 'Medieval Programme' made them more sought-after as carpenters, and, as a result, the programme contributed to the

Figure 5.11   Repairing a medieval storehouse in Tokke, Norway. The structure is repaired in situ without dismantling. New, well-seasoned wood is jointed in

survival of local communities. The carpenters involved in the programme were either self-employed or employed by a local contractor, the purpose being to build up an infrastructure of craftsmen rather than establish a permanent organisation, such as a permanent workshop. Thus, after its completion the infrastructure of the 'Medieval Programme' could survive in other types of conservation work.

Through articles and announcements in the local press and in local agricultural associ-

Figure 5.12 Cleaved shingles in one of the 'material banks' established as part of the programme to repair medieval timber structures in Norway, 1991–96

the heartwood being used. Timber of similar quality for repair work was bought by the Directorate in quantities that were larger than were needed for the actual project. As a result, the Directorate was able to establish stores of building materials for repair work in six regions in southern Norway. These stores, or 'material banks' as they are called, contain materials such as pine (round and sawn), various forms of shingles (cleaved, planed and sawed), roof tiles and birch bark for roofing. The stores also carry tools which are too expensive for local carpenters to invest in, like hydraulic jacks which are used to lift the heavy weights of complete buildings, or to lift part of log walls in order to insert repair pieces or whole new logs. Some of the carpenters who have been involved in the programme are responsible for the maintenance of the six regional stores. The idea of maintaining reserves of appropriate quality materials for preservation work is recommended in Article 12 of the Wood Committee's Principles:

> *Institutions responsible for the preservation and conservation of historic structures and sites should establish or encourage the establishment of stores of timber appropriate for such work.*

To meet the demands of the Norwegian 'Medieval Programme', subsidiary suppliers of special materials and special tools were also employed, in addition to carpenters and other professional craftsmen. In many cases these were local farmers, who thus acquired an extra source of income. Products include traditionally distilled pine tar, birch bark for roofing, special types of wood products, hand-made nails and various types of shingles. Local blacksmiths were hired to produce tools, such as plane blades. Small local water-powered frame saws and water-driven shingle planes were repaired and

ation newsletters, the Directorate for Cultural Heritage came into contact with forest owners and others who could supply materials. The programme was based on close co-operation with national and local forest authorities and owners for the delivery of timber of a suitable quality for the programme. This work will probably have a significant impact on future preservation work on timber structures in the various regions of the country. The medieval buildings were built from large pines, with only

Figure 5.13 St Nicolas Chapel, Kenozero National Park, Archangel, Russia, was restored in 1995–96 by Russian and Norwegian carpenters. The repair of the chapel is one of several joint Russian–Norwegian projects aimed at preservation of historic timber buildings through the revival of traditional techniques of craftsmanship. Hydraulic jacks and steel posts made it possible to renew rotten horizontal logs, while at the same time avoiding dismantling the chapel. (Photo by Anders Haslestad, Directorate for Cultural Heritage, Norway)

Figure 5.14 A Norwegian blacksmith making traditional carpentry tools

restored, together with the waterways and dams that provide hydropower. It was hoped that when it became known locally that such products were available on the market, other people would use them to repair their houses, and these materials also could be used in contemporary construction of small houses. In this way a small permanent market could be created for these special products, thereby helping to preserve the traditional crafts on which they were based for the future.

The programme contributed significantly to perfecting the abilities of the carpenters and craftsmen who were involved in working with historic buildings of high value. It was intended that the techniques and approaches to repair learnt by the craftsmen involved in this programme could also be applied to other types of historic buildings. The project therefore contributed to this through training carpenters and other craftsmen, who might later be asked to join particularly demanding projects in their home regions. Until the completion of the 'Medieval Programme', this had been a major problem all over Norway.

A co-ordinated effort such as the Norwegian 'Medieval Programme' has obvious advantages. It is possible for a country to build up an infrastructure that will also benefit conservation work in general, in local districts or regions. The success of the Norwegian 'Medieval Programme' also depended on a relatively generous contribution from the Ministry of the Environment for the preservation of those timber structures which were automatically listed under the Cultural Heritage Act.

The 'Medieval Programme' is an example of how a government policy for regional development may be put into practice. Many of the carpenters involved in the programme have acquired an increased workload after participating in the programme of repair work of historic buildings. At the same time

Figure 5.15 A frame saw in Rauland, Norway, which was restored together with the associated waterways and dams as part of the Medieval Programme in Norway, 1991–96

they are also active in erecting new timber structures in their own district, thus bringing their knowledge of sound craft techniques into contemporary construction work. Their contact with restoration and repair work has given them new opportunities and a deeper understanding of buildings that are ecologically sound and also adapted to the local climatic and physical conditions. As craftsmen they can offer a high-quality alternative to the standardised approach of the contemporary building industry based on prefabricated elements.

6

Mighty oaks from little acorns grow: preservation starts in the forest

There inevitably comes a time when the replacement of members is necessary in an historic timber structure. These members may have decayed or become degraded due to fungi or insect attacks, or they may have deteriorated or been destroyed by physical causes, such as fire. To preserve existing timber structures, or to reconstruct timber structures after a fire, new timber of an appropriate quality will be needed to replace deteriorated or destroyed parts. The first requirement of new timber is that it should be of the same species and have material properties and dimensions compatible with the original material.

Today, it is becoming increasingly difficult and even impossible in many countries to find timber of a quality that matches the historic material. The reasons for this may be that the proper forest resources have not yet been identified, or timber of appropriate quality is not available at all because the forest resources have been depleted, or the appropriate quality timber may not be obtainable on the market. If we lack suitable timber we also lack the chance to preserve the authenticity of our wooden cultural heritage.

The lack of timber of adequate dimensions is not, however, a new phenomenon. In fact, lack of sufficiently large or long timbers has been a driving force throughout history in the devel-

opment of timber engineering. By the end of the Roman Empire, the spanning limitations of readily available timber led to the development of the simple truss for roofing purposes. During the Middle Ages, lack of large-dimension timber for joists led to ingenious solutions for floor constructions. During the Renaissance, arches were constructed from shorter and slender members, such as planks, and this was also applied to beam construction (Mainstone, 1975: 138–140).

6.1 Historic Forest Reserves

How is timber of the right quality to be found both today and in the future for preservation work? In 1992, the ICOMOS International Wood Committee organised an international symposium in Nepal to discuss the preservation of timber structures and wood used in buildings in connection with the Kathmandu Valley World Heritage Site (Larsen and Marstein, 1994a). The symposium greatly helped the Committee to see the need for forest resources that can supply timber for the repair and restoration of historic structures: the native hardwood – sal (*Shorea robusta*) – used in the original construction work was scarce, and the softwoods used instead were of extremely poor quality.

Figure 6.1 Large dimension timber from a late sixteenth-century log structure in Setesdal, Norway

Figure 6.2 Softwood used in Nepalese preservation work. The width of the annual rings is approximately one centimetre. The amount of heartwood was almost negligible

As a result, the Wood Committee proposes in Article 12 of the Principles the establishment and protection of forest or woodland reserves – 'Historic Forest Reserves' – from which appropriate timber can be obtained for the preservation and repair of cultural heritage made of wood. The Wood Committee has proposed that projects implemented under the banner of Historic Forest Reserves should include, firstly, finding and protecting existing natural forests that contain historic species of the maturity traditionally required for construction work, and, secondly, enrich-

ment planting to restore species that may have been depleted by over-utilisation.

However, it is not only developing countries, like Nepal, which suffer from a lack of forest resources where suitable timber may be found. For example, experts in the UK have recognised that the forest resources which yielded large oak timbers used in days gone by for roof trusses, for example, have now virtually disappeared. Thus, old, large structural members cannot usually be replaced. During the restoration of the York Minster tower in 1970, the original, decayed

Figure 6.3 Pine with large section of heartwood in one of the Norwegian 'material banks' set up during the Medieval Programme in Norway, 1991–96

members were so large that the conservation architect, despite approaching every timber merchant in the UK, could find only one tree that was big enough to provide replacement members of a similar size. The architect was, reluctantly, forced to replace the original timber structure with steel lattice beams (Charles, 1984: 47).

In Norway, the implications of the concept of Historic Forest Reserves became evident in the 'Medieval Programme' managed by the Directorate for Cultural Heritage. One of the key issues in the programme became the establishment of stores, called 'material banks', for traditional building materials in various regions throughout the country. A major asset in the banks is old-growth pine (*Pinus sylvestris*), carefully selected in co-

operation with local forest owners, and matching the quality of the timber used in the original construction work. There is a growing interest among forest owners to keep similar reserves in the future.

The idea of establishing forest reserves for construction purposes is not, however, a novel idea. A spectacular example of an old system is forest management in the Venetian Republic – *la Serenissima*. An important motive in the Republic's westward expansion in the fourteenth and fifteenth centuries was the need to secure a steady supply of oak timber for the Venetian shipbuilding industry, and also timber for construction work. Timber was needed for the piled foundations under buildings, floor and roof structures in private and public buildings, and to prevent erosion of the Venetian lagoon. As early as the fifteenth century, the Republic had developed an advanced forestry policy based on the understanding that the wealth of the Republic actually started in the forests. The laws and regulations drawn up to defend and develop the forests were aimed at what in modern terms would be referred to as the preservation of the ecological equilibrium of the forests (Ministero per i Beni Culturali e Ambientali, 1987; Susmel, 1994).

The Wood Committee's proposal for the establishment of Historic Forest Reserves links cultural heritage preservation with nature conservation. The Wood Committee would like to tie cultural heritage preservation to broader ecological concerns under the aegis of the World Heritage concept. By regarding heritage as both cultural and natural, the World Heritage Convention reminds the international community of the interaction between people and nature and of the fundamental need to preserve the balance between people and the environment. Our responsibility as conservators of cultural heritage made of wood is, therefore, not only limited to timber structures but also extends to the conservation and sustainable use of forest resources. Since current forestry policies and management techniques create the fundamental conditions for the preservation of timber structures using authentic materials, both now and for the future, we must understand the nature of these policies and silvicultural techniques exactly, and, if necessary, strive to change them if they are contrary to the needs of cultural heritage preservation.

6.2 Sustained yield management and sustainable management of forests

Forests form an integral part of life on earth, providing a range of benefits at local, national and regional levels, covering approximately 40 per cent of the world's total land mass, according to a 1995 survey of the United Nations Food and Agriculture Organisation (FAO). During the past two centuries, the exploitation of these rich resources has been dominated by the idea of sustainable yield management. This idea was based on harvesting old-growth forests through clear-felling at the same rate as new wood was formed by growth processes. It was assumed that this state could be maintained indefinitely through forest management without negative effects.

In the sustained yield forestry management system, clear-felling was followed by artificial reforestation with tree species of economic importance. In the course of time, however, soil scientists and ecologists have found that clear-felling had considerable drawbacks. Although clear-felling obviously has economic and management advantages, it is also burdened with ecological and biological risks. The on-going evolution from sustained-yield management of a relatively small number of commercial tree species to the protection and sustainable management of forest ecosystems is changing some of the fundamental premises of forest management.

Today, it is recognised that forests are complex ecosystems capable of providing a wide range of economic, social and environmental benefits. Ecosystems are communities of organisms working together with their environments as integrated units. They are places where all plants, animals, soils, waters, climate, people and processes of life interact as a whole.

A school of European forestry has long advocated silvicultural systems based on natural woodland. There is a developing body of opinion that in the long-term we will best protect the productive potential of forests for timber if we stay as close as possible to a natural system of management. Site

Figure 6.4   Detail of logs in a Norwegian log structure from the late eighteenth century. Note the extremely narrow width of the annual rings

nutrient status, freedom from disease, even the growth form of individual trees may be better in mixed forests with a full, natural rotation of age-classes. Natural regeneration may be a cheaper and more practicable method of restocking after felling (Peterken, 1996). In forestry today, a major challenge is to develop more creative silvicultural techniques which provide for long-term commodity production and the maintenance of biodiversity. Increasing uneven-aged management of many forest types and implementing longer periods of rotation in even-

aged systems are current topics in the forestry debate. Selection felling is regarded as the logical low-impact alternative to clear-felling but is not necessarily a solution in all cases. Selection felling involves the removal of single or small groups of trees within a stand. Selection felling, applied uniformly to the landscape, may have not desirable ecological consequences or may be inappropriate under certain site conditions, such as unstable soils and steep topography, because of the need for extensive roads and frequent felling.

6.3 Forests, the 1992 Rio Earth Summit and its aftermath

Public interest and concern for the health and well-being of the world's forests have never been greater. For this reason, concern about forestry's evolving roles became the subject of intense debate at the United Nations Conference on Environment and Development in 1992 (the Rio Earth Summit). The conference highlighted forestry development and environmental issues by developing a set of 'Forest Principles' and devoting a chapter of its programme of action, 'Agenda 21', to combating deforestation. The Forest Principles affirm that it is essential for both environmental and economic well-being that the growing and felling of trees leave soils, water and ecosystems in diverse and productive conditions.

One initiative following the Rio Earth Summit has been the process of developing and implementing criteria and indicators for sustainable forest management. More than 100 countries in six continents, accounting for most of the world's forests as well as international trade in forest products, are involved in the debate. Globally there are currently seven initiatives, known as 'processes', which aim to develop criteria and indicators for sustainable forest management within specific regions. Within the 'Helsinki Process', covering Europe, sustainable forest management is defined as the stewardship and use of forests and forest lands in a way, and at a rate, that maintains their biodiversity, productivity, regeneration capacity, vitality and their potential to fulfil, now and in the future, relevant ecological, economic and social functions, at local, national and global levels, without causing damage to other ecosystems. The preservation of historic timber structures will certainly benefit from this policy to promote sustainable forestry practices, if not immediately, then in the long term.

6.4 Forest conservation

The issue of forest conservation creates fierce controversies and arouses strong feelings. Conservationists appear to be at odds with forest owners, foresters and the public, who see the need for a steady flow of appropriate forest resources, including timber, to the market. The central issue is the conservation of biological diversity – **biodiversity**. Biodiversity is defined simply as the level of variety and variation in the ecosystem, species and genetic levels.

However, biological diversity is but one of several parameters by which a natural resource can be described. Other parameters include structure or biological productivity, for example. The 1992 Rio Summit and its aftermath have generated such awareness of the term biodiversity that it seems to overshadow other related problems. Emphasis on the perceived value of inherent biodiversity attributes versus the direct value of the resources themselves fuels international and national debates. To what extent should forests be maintained for their production or protection value? Can a forest be managed for both purposes? Biodiversity literature stresses the level of our ignorance

as to the extent of community, species and genetic diversity: at the component level (how many species are there, and where?) and at the structural and functional levels (how does this assembly of species function in terms of carbon storage, etc.?). A fundamental question that may critically be added to this is how much biodiversity do we need – because we cannot have everything (Rodgers, 1997).

We would agree with the views of George F. Peterken (1996), that modern wilderness preservation is based on separation of people and nature – conceptually and physically. Nature is only visited, not experienced in everyday life, and this approach contains the seeds of its own downfall. There is a feeling of alienation from nature within urban society and an urge to re-establish contact, but this against a background belief that people are a disrupting force outside nature. Foresters, according to Peterken, have tended to regard natural or unmanaged woodland as a wasted resource; nature conservationists have generally seen it as an ideal. Foresters have been trained to grow trees and to manage woodland actively. Conservationists exist to promote, among other things, natural features and processes, and so they have tended to interfere as little as possible.

However, there is a higher register of protection and nature conservation aims, although this is not as yet fully acknowledged world-wide. This is the Protected Areas Category System of IUCN, the World Conservation Union. IUCN classifies protection in six categories, and Category 6 is of particular relevance for Historic Forest Reserves. This category is called 'Managed Resource Protected Area: protected area managed mainly for the sustainable use of natural ecosystems'. This is defined as an area containing predominantly unmodified natural systems, managed to ensure long-term protection and maintenance of biological diversity, while providing at the same time a sustainable flow of natural products and services to meet community needs. The objectives are four-fold:

1. to protect and maintain the biological diversity and other natural values of the area in the long term;
2. to promote sound management practices for sustainable production purposes;
3. to protect the natural resource base from being alienated for other land-use purposes that would be detrimental to the area's biological diversity;
4. to contribute to regional and national development.

The use of this category in nature conservation policy may serve to eliminate many of the controversies we see today, and at the same time maintain each country's obligations to international conventions, such as the convention on biodiversity, while at the same time securing timber for architectural preservation as well as other worthy purposes.

In the future, when the concept of ecosystem forestry management has matured and eventually been implemented, there should be a steady and secure supply of timber of adequate quality for architectural preservation work. Until then, the concept of Historic Forest Reserves may help to remind forest owners and managers to keep parts of the remaining old-growth forests for the sake of preserving the authenticity of the world's historic timber structures.

Figure 6.5 A straight-grown pine to be felled by the carpenter, selected on the basis of its bark and straight growth, making it suitable for cleaving

6.5 Traditional knowledge of tree selection in the forest

When carpenters in the northern European coniferous area were to build timber structures, such as churches, they went out into the forest and selected the individual trees needed for this purpose. The individual forester or carpenter had, through his own experience, established a knowledge of timber quality that far surpassed the expert systems being developed in today's forestry to predict wood quality. Traditional knowledge indicated special stands that people knew would provide excellent materials for construction purposes. Most attractive, in their eyes, were the 'mature' pines because of their high content of heartwood, which made the timbers stable in use and highly resistant to decay. A mature tree could be distinguished according to several criteria, such as the shape and size of the trunk, height and diameter increase and the appearance of the bark and knots.

To choose the right size of tree, the forester or carpenter started out with the dimensions of the element for which the tree was needed: the size of beams or posts, or the logs for a log-wall. The guiding principle was to fell trees no bigger than were needed. This seems to have been a universal approach to the selection of trees for structural purposes. Fred Charles observes the same approach to tree felling from the English oak forests. For reasons of economy, the carpenter selected the smallest tree that would yield the required cross-section of the structural member (Charles, 1984: 47).

In Scandinavia, trees were traditionally felled during autumn and winter. It was easier to haul the logs out of the forest at this time of year, because the ground was frozen and snow-covered. Moreover, the life-processes of the trees were halted, and the danger of fungal decay in the newly felled trees was eliminated. Ancient Chinese carpenters also knew that wood felled in winter was comparatively dry and strong and did not rot easily (Zhong and Chen, 1986: 303). In Oppdal, a Norwegian mountain village, up until the late 1930s building timber was always felled during September. In the spring it was hewn on two sides and left to dry during summer, stacked so that it was exposed to the air on all sides. During the autumn, the log house was erected and roofed, and then left over the winter. Weighed down by the snow, the log walls became very tight. The windows and doors were put in during the summer, and the inhabitants could move in. In this way they made a house that could last for centuries and would be weather-tight, providing comfortable interior conditions during the very cold winters (Vreim, 1948: 33).

The traditional knowledge of tree selection for construction work is gradually being lost. We might ask how useful this knowledge is today, since the forest resources upon which such traditional knowledge was based are, in many places, depleted. Seen in the broader perspective of evolving ideas in international forestry, there are, however, promising signs of a growing interest in preserving and even re-establishing the patterns of the world's old-growth forests from which our ancestors developed their knowledge and where they could select the best trees for building purposes. It should therefore be a fundamental duty for those who are concerned with the preservation of the authenticity of the world's historic timber structures, to make clear society's need for high-quality old-growth timber for preservation work, and to study the methods and techniques that were traditionally used to select timber for building purposes. This implies that architectural conservators must be thoroughly schooled in the traditional as well as in the current principles of forestry practice.

7

A little neglect may breed mischief: preventive conservation, documentation, maintenance and fire protection

Since the 1980s, preventive conservation has become a major tool in museum conservation, with the realisation that the daily routine work of maintaining museum environments and, in particular, a stable climate, actually prevents decay and deterioration of museum artefacts. Although the term preventive conservation has only rarely been applied to architectural conservation, it is obvious that maintenance of buildings is a form of preventive conservation. Fire protection of buildings also falls into the category of preventive conservation. We would like to suggest that the inspection and recording of buildings are also parts of a preventive conservation strategy. Firstly, it is of vital importance to document a timber structure in case of damage, for instance, caused by fire. Secondly, careful inspection may reduce interventions when repair seems inevitable. Thirdly, inspection of buildings at regular intervals is a fundamental part of a maintenance programme.

7.1 Inspection and recording

Historic timber structures will inevitably show evidence of decline. In addition to natural causes, buildings may have suffered the effects of fire, war damage, earlier unsuccessful intervention measures or may have been put to inappropriate use. In order to make a proper appraisal of the current state of an historic timber structure, an inspection of the structure alone will not suffice. A more comprehensive record, including a whole range of issues concerning the past and present condition of the structure and its environment, needs to be made. For example, when treating a decayed timber member, we need to understand the reasons that caused it to decay, and these decay-causing factors need to be removed, or treated, before we treat the actual member.

In practical terms this implies that before any action is taken, it is necessary to have a thorough understanding of the structure and its history. This also implies that the situation should be monitored over a period of time in order to determine whether or not it is necessary to take action or whether the structure may be left as it is for the present. If possible, the monitoring period should be in excess of one year in order to take account of ordinary seasonal variations in, for instance, movements in the structure (Brereton, 1995: 13). Having thus inspected, recorded and

(a)

(b)

Figure 7.1 (a) A warehouse at Kjerringøy, Norway, from the early nineteenth century. Salt fish had been stored here for years. This led to salt erosion of the timber in the foundations. (b) Detail of salt-eroded timber

monitored the structure, and studied its history, the conservator will have a solid platform from which to make decisions about what intervention measures are necessary.

Inspection, recording and documentation are covered by Articles 1 and 2 of the Wood Committee's Principles. Moreover, the Principles refer to, and are based on, Article 16 of the Venice Charter and a separate ICOMOS document dealing with the recording of historic buildings. The Wood Committee's Principles recommend the secure storage of all documentation material, and include in this redundant materials and members removed from the structure during repair work. Such members should be kept as valuable historic records for future research. Further, the Wood Committee emphasises that it is essential to record information about relevant traditional skills and technologies.

7.2 The Venice Charter and the ICOMOS recording principles

Recording is an essential part of the conservation process. According to the Principles for the Recording of Monuments, Groups of Buildings and Sites, adopted by the ICOMOS General Assembly in 1996, recording can be defined as the capture of information that describes the physical configuration, condition and use of the monuments, groups of buildings and sites, at different points in time.

Recording is essential, *inter alia*, to ensure the informed management and control of construction works and of all changes to cultural heritage, and to provide information that can be used to identify appropriate and sustainable use. Recording should be undertaken before, during and after repairs, alterations or other interventions, and when evidence of a building's history is revealed during such works. The ICOMOS recording principles emphasise that the recording and interpretation processes are complex and may require several professional groups to work together, such as architects, conservators, engineers, surveyors, architectural historians, archaeologists above and below ground, and other specialist advisers.

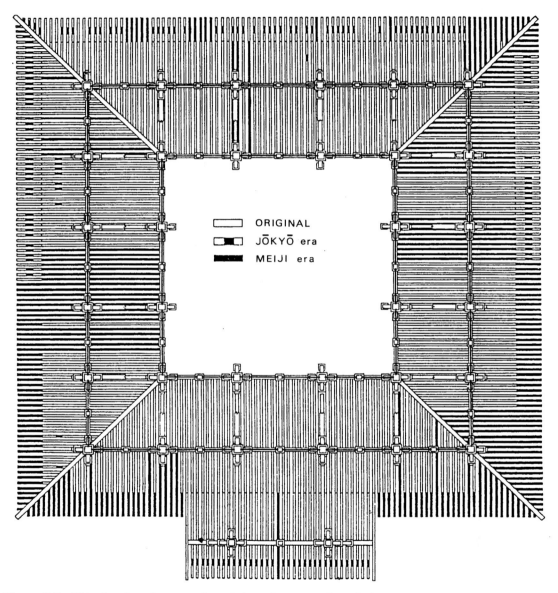

Figure 7.2   This drawing shows a plan of the rafters seen from below in the *Jôgyôdô* hall of the Enryaku-ji Buddhist temple in Shiga, Japan. The hall was built in 1595. The drawing shows the original members, and members added during repairs in the late seventeenth and late nineteenth century. (Drawing from *Juyo bunkazai Enryakuji jogyodo oyobi hokkedo shuri koji hokokusho*, Shiga Prefecture Board of Education, 1968)

A complete record of an historic structure as a basis for conservation work comprises a comprehensive set of information pertaining to the building's history and its present state. It should include:

1. measured drawings;
2. photographs;
3. building history, including repair history;
4. documentation of the present physical condition of the building or structure in question.

Evidence that may explain the construction history, and, in particular the previous use of crafts techniques and tools, should be particularly noted. Access to all the information about a cultural resource is a key to its protection and presentation.

The ICOMOS recording principles are based on the recommendation of Article 16 in the Venice Charter, which clearly states that recording is an ongoing process during actual repair work:

In all works of preservation, restoration, or excavation, there should always be precise documentation in the form of analytical and critical reports, illustrated with drawings and photographs.

Every stage of the work of clearing, consolidation, rearrangement and integration, as well as technical and formal features identified during the course of the work, should be included. This record should be placed in the archives of a public institution and made available to research workers. It is recommended that the report should be published. The Japanese have developed an extremely conscientious approach to the recording of historic buildings before, during and after repair work, completely in accordance with Article 16 of the Venice Charter. Moreover, the Japanese always publish a report of the records upon completion of a major repair project of a listed building. The reports are distributed to conservation architects, and to the main libraries all over Japan and internationally. Expenses for publication of the report are included in the total budget for the repair project (Larsen, 1994: 138–143). The reports convey a detailed account of the various aspects of the project, such as:

1. the work schedule, budget and all extra work on site, including construction of the site office and scaffolding;
2. the building and its history, based on the evidence found prior to and during the work;
3. the repair process, including the method for repair of individual members.

All items are described through text, diagrams, drawings and photographs.

The Japanese reports on repair work address two major issues. Firstly, the reports remain primary sources of architectural history. Secondly, the reports account for every aspect of the repair project, from construction of scaffolding to woodwork joints used in the repair work, which benefits future planning. Based on the information contained in the reports, it is possible to estimate the costs and the working hours which are necessary for the various operations in future projects. These reports are of great interest, not only from a Japanese perspective, as they could also serve as a prototype for preservation experts everywhere who are intent on meeting their obligations to the Venice Charter.

7.3 Documentation of building history

The documentation and analysis of building history are essential parts of the conservation

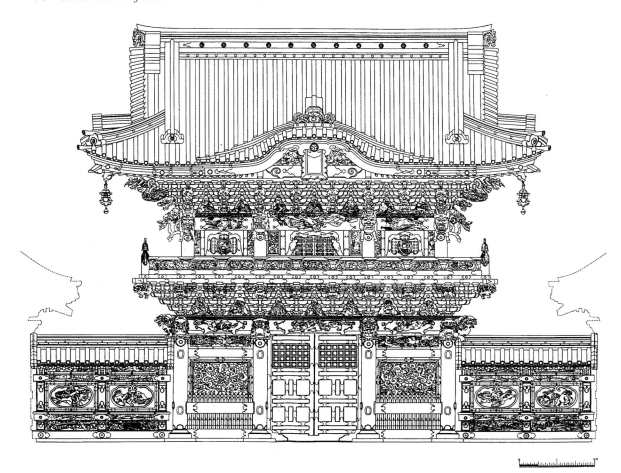

Figure 7.3 Drawing from the report of repair work at the Main Gate of the Toshogu shrine in Nikko, Japan. (Drawing from *Kokuho Toshogu yomeimon shuri koji hokokusho*, The Foundation for the Preservation of Cultural Heritage in the Shrines and Temples of Nikko,1974)

process. Clarification of the building history is a necessary condition for the elaboration of a proper concept of the conservation, and in particular when interventions in the building or structure are deemed inevitable. Only through archival research and an actual examination of the structure is it possible to recognise and analyse the historical resources that are represented in it. Such research and analysis should precede any intervention. Since much of the significance of the building or structure is attached to its material substance, and since we wish to retain as much of this documentary evidence as possible, we must understand its significance.

Moreover, through the research and analysis of building and structural history, we will be able to determine previous repairs and to understand the effects, structural or otherwise, of earlier interventions. Experience proves that there is always a close connection between the historical development of a building or structure and the development of damage, decay or deterioration. Frequently, if the judgement of damage or deterioration is limited to current observations but does not

Figure 7.4 The pilgrimage church of Wies near Steingaden, Bavaria, Germany, is a World Heritage Site. It was built between 1745 and 1754. The church, situated in an alpine valley, is a masterpiece of rococo art and architecture. The masonry church walls and eight paired pillars carry a timbered roof structure and a wooden vault over the central area (the nave). The vault consists of ribs suspended in the roof structure, a construction typical of baroque churches. Laths are nailed to the ribs. The vault soffit is plastered and painted with beautiful frescoes. As the vault is linked to the roof structure, all forces affecting the roof, such as wind, consequently affect the vault and its stucco decorations.

Damages linked to frequent flights of military aircraft over the church in 1984 led to the church being closed out of concern for the safety of visitors. However, due to extensive inspection and comprehensive analysis of the structure and its history, the Bavarian State Conservation Office realised that it was not necessary to intervene in the delicate roof structure. Instead a system of monitoring was established. The structure could be conserved as it was, on the condition that a plan for future regular inspections was implemented

take into account the historical development of the structure, it is likely that the evaluation of the problem and the proposed remedies will not be relevant or appropriate. Of course, if the decay is limited to penetration of water at a specific point, historical analysis is necessarily not required, but if the problem is more comprehensive, for example related to structural damage, historical research and analysis are certainly prerequisites for finding the appropriate measures to cope with the problem.

7.4 Survey and analysis of physical condition defects

We are unlikely to find a globally applicable survey checklist for tracing defects and damage in historic timber structures, because the issue is so complex, taking into account the diversity of forms of timber structures, wood species, climatic and geographical conditions. Survey checklists must be adapted to the types of structures in question, and the local and regional climatic and other

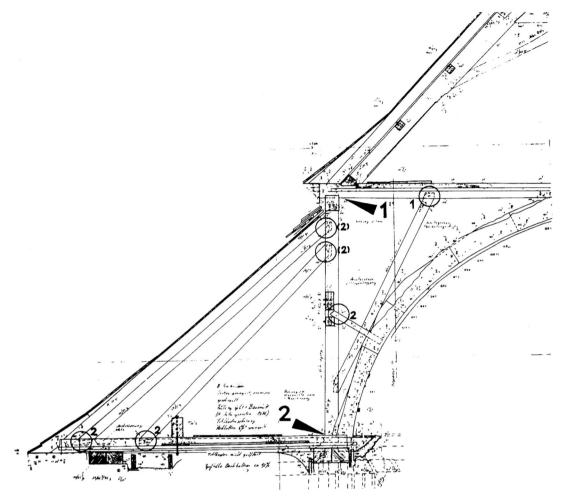

Figure 7.5   Wies church in Bavaria, Germany. Section of the roof. (Drawing from *Die Wies. Geschichte und Restaurierung,* Bayerisches Landesamt für Denkmalpflege, Arbeitsheft 55, München, 1992; p. 135)

environmental conditions. Therefore, only local conservators will have sufficiently good knowledge and insight into where and how to find the trouble-spots in historic timber structures and consequently how to compile a relevant defects survey checklist. Weaver (1993: 36–39) has suggested an extensive checklist which may be an excellent starting point for developing local or site-specific lists.

Exact measured drawings are the most helpful tools in conservation work in general,

and specifically in the defects survey. Exact drawings may show deformations and possible structural problems. Moreover, the architectural conservator can directly plot damaged or decayed areas onto the drawing. This will give an immediate impression of the extent of the damage and whether there are areas of the building or structure that should be given special attention.

Measuring and recording historic buildings is, however, a time-consuming process. A 3D database may greatly simplify the documenta-

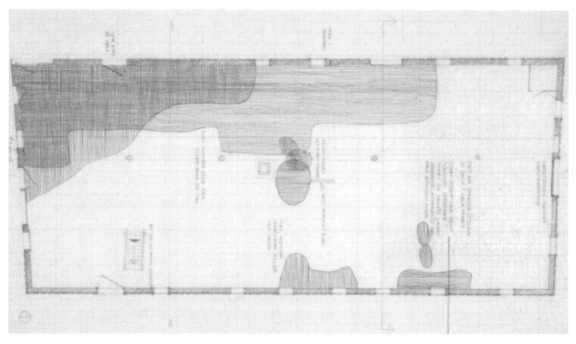

Figure 7.6 A measured drawing with decay and damage indicated

tion and recording process. Today, laser scanners and computer programs that allow the construction of 3D models in real time while working in the field, are available. All the other necessary information, such as building history and the physical condition, can be added to the model. However, it is beyond the scope of this book to deal with the vast range of new technology for effective recording and information retrieval. The proceedings of the symposia of the ICOMOS International Committee for Architectural Photogrammetry offer valuable and updated information in this field.

In any case, whether the architectural conservator is working with traditional recording tools or with sophisticated computer systems, it is necessary to use all the senses when examining or inspecting a timber structure for damage and decay: sight, hearing, smell and touch, and, in some cases,

even taste. Sometimes conservators may be able to see the fruiting bodies or the mycelium of fungi on the surface of timbers, or bore holes or bore dust from insects. By knocking on wood it is possible to judge from the sound whether the timber is sound or not. The mouldy smell of an ongoing fungal attack is usually easily perceived. Conservators should feel the wood to check if the surface feels damp. When the purpose is to determine structural as well as material damage, deterioration or decay, the quality of the end result depends on the conservator's ability to work as systematically as possible.

In any timber structure, there will be obvious trouble-spots where water, the main enemy of wood, may penetrate surfaces or accumulate on horizontal surfaces and in timber embedded in masonry, and thus lead to fungal decay. Water stains are the first indication that something is wrong. Obvious

(a)

Figure 7.7 (a) The 'Wooden Pagoda' of Fogong Temple in Yin county, Shanxi, China, built in 1056. The height of the pagoda is 66 metres, including the 10 metre high iron spire. (b) Wooden members which have been crushed due to the heavy weight of the pagoda

(b)

Figure 7.8 Lichen growing on the surface of timber exposed to the weather. This is not necessarily dangerous in itself, but large amounts of lichen may accumulate moisture and create conditions for fungal decay

places for close inspection are timbers in contact with or near the ground, such as sill beams or posts. Unventilated spaces beneath wooden floors at ground level should be given special attention.

Unfortunately, leaks in the roofs of buildings happen frequently. If not arrested, they may lead to decay in the roof timbers. Particularly problematic is timber under valleys in roofs. The junction between rafters and beams at the eaves, where the walls meet the roof, is a notorious trouble-spot because damage in this area may be caused by humidity, as well as by loading, and often the rafters, as well as the beams, may be decayed or damaged.

Crevices, cracks or openings in joints are favourite entry spots for insects and should be carefully observed. Exit holes of insects in timbers and bore dust on the floor are obvious signs of an insect attack. However, until further observation has been carried out, it will not be possible to ascertain whether the attack is current or not. When inspecting for possible insect attacks, it is extremely important to be systematic and observant, and to plot all relevant information onto the measured drawings.

Whenever possible, the conservation architect, the carpenter and other professionals such as a structural engineer or a mycologist, should survey the structure together. This offers an excellent opportunity for them not only to learn how to understand the structure itself, but also to understand each other's work. This may greatly simplify future collaboration during repair work.

Figure 7.9 A moisture meter

7.4.1 Simple inspection tools

Probing wood with a penknife or a similar tool, such as an awl, will normally indicate whether the damage by infestation or fungal attack is significant or not. If the knife-blade or awl disappears easily into the wood, it is obviously not sound. However, one should not always rely on the probing method, because just inside the sound wood, the central part may be decayed, as is sometimes the case for timber embedded in masonry.

Sounding with a hammer or mallet is an efficient way to find out whether wood is sound. If there is a dead sound, the wood is decayed or has been attacked by insects. Moreover, beetle holes may appear, and fresh bore dust or frass may come out of the holes due to the vibration when the wood is tapped.

An extremely useful and simple tool to use in diagnosing fungal decay is the moisture meter. Fungal decay will occur if the moisture content of the wood is at or above fibre saturation point, which, depending on the species of wood, is around 25–30 per cent. Typically, insect attacks also occur at high moisture levels, but there is not necessarily a strict correlation. A moisture meter is a small electrical instrument which operates on the principle that wet wood is an excellent conductor of electricity while dry wood is a very good insulator. It is normally based on the direct electrical resistance of the wood. By driving pin-type electrodes into the wood, the resistance is measured and converted into moisture content values by the instrument. To obtain proper readings from a moisture meter, it is essential that the pins are driven into the wood in their full depth. Driving the pins in at sufficient depth is not always easy with the denser woods.

Moisture meters are calibrated by the manufacturer for a given species of a given thickness at a given temperature. When measuring moisture content in a sample, it is therefore important to refer to the manufacturer's recommended conversion table regarding correction factors for various species. However, more sophisticated moisture meters have small plug-in program keys which automatically set the calibration required for different species.

7.4.2 Instruments and tools for non-destructive testing of wood in structures

There are also several mechanical instruments on the market which are highly useful when surveying building timbers. Generally, these instruments have been developed for use in forestry operations, but their application to historic buildings surveys is obvious.

An excellent tool is the decay-detecting drill, which allows accurate assessment of the structural integrity of timbers. The principle of operation of one such drill is that, at constant drilling pressure, a long, narrow, flexible, telescopically supported drill bit, rotated at high speed, rapidly penetrates the wood. This simultaneously produces a graphic record of the rate of penetration. Decay or insect attack is detected by a sudden change in bandwidth between the lines on the trace record. The marked reduction in density and the nature of the spacing will show whether the damage is caused by decay or by insect attack. The small diameter drill leaves a virtually undetectable test hole, resulting in no structural damage to the timber.

Another tool used in forestry practice that may be used by building conservators is the electronic hammer. This is an instrument that measures the time it takes for a sound wave to pass through a tree. Each species of wood has its own characteristic sound velocity. Deviations from this indicate cavities or decay in the wood. The sound velocity measured is either shown on a hand-held display connected to the hammer, or the instrument may be equipped with a printer. Moreover, the electronic hammer allows the modulus of elasticity of logs, as well as building timber, to be assessed.

Non-destructive testing can also be done with the help of infrared light, ultrasound and endoscopy. Ultrasonic inspection methods, using a pulse velocity measuring device, developed initially for testing concrete, have shown promising results in detecting decay in building timbers (Lee, 1970; Baldassino *et al.*, 1996). Structural endoscopy allows visual inspection of places that are not accessible, such as the inside of walls, floors and ceilings. Apart from visual inspection, specimens from non-accessible areas can be collected using special tools.

Infrared spectrometry has been successfully used to investigate timber-framed structures that have been plastered, thus establishing a survey of the condition of the actual timber frame without the need to destroy layers of plaster. Infrared thermography is a convenient technique for producing heat images from the invisible radiant energy emitted from an object at any distance, without surface contact and without in any way influencing the actual surface temperature of the objects viewed. For this work, a scanning camera is used. This method gives a measure of material damage and permits the evaluation of the progressive damaging processes under load. However, the use of this method presupposes a temperature gradient between the outside and the inside of the building (Luong, 1996).

7.5 Structural survey and engineering calculations

Engineering calculations can be invaluable in evaluating the strength of structures and of eroded timbers in difficult cases. However, prior to any repair of timbered roof structures, the following facts concerning the development of the structural framework should be considered:

1. how the structure tolerates the loads imposed on it;
2. what kinds of loads (tension, compression, bending or combinations of these) the individual members are subjected to;

3. how the joints are affected by the loads; and

4. what loads the roof structure transfers to its environment (walls, tier of joists, etc.) and where the loads are transferred.

The answers to these questions present a complete picture of the structural mechanics. For a particular roof structure, several different models of its structural mechanics may be set up. The consequences of the distribution of loads and forces internally in the structure and on the environment may differ from model to model. One would usually opt for the model that respects the existing structure to the largest extent, and that minimises the need for interventions and utilises the present structural possibilities as far as possible (Troelsgård, 1995).

7.6 Structural survey and timber grading

A simple way of assessing structural timber quality is to use present-day grading rules for determining the load-bearing capacity of each individual member in a structure. This is not to say that structural timbers in an historic structure must comply with present-day grading rules, and particularly not if the member is functioning properly. However, grading using present-day rules and included as a part of the structural survey, gives an indication of the structural reliability of the timbers.

Grading is the process of classifying timber according to quality for a particular use. Grading of some sort has always been a necessary part of carpentry. Carpenters knew well the effect of certain growth characteristics or defects in timber and good craftsmen selected their timber carefully to obtain the required quality. When sawmills were manually operated, the workers were highly

Figure 7.10 From a sawmill in Sakurai city, Nara, Japan. This sawmill specialises in Japanese cypress (*Chamaecyparis obtusa*). The ends of each log are waxed to stabilise the humidity inside the wood. Cramps are inserted into the ends to avoid cracking

skilled in evaluating the quality of the material and could sort timbers, boards and planks for specific use during the conversion process.

Visual grading is the successor to the sorting done by the workers at a traditional small sawmill. The grader examines each piece to determine the type, location and size of various growth characteristics that may affect its structural strength, and considers wood density and the ratio of heartwood to sapwood. Then, using rules that quantify the effect of each characteristic, the grader assigns the piece a 'grade' by stamping it with a grade stamp. Strength-reducing characteris-

Figure 7.11 The Mountain Resort, Chengde, China, a World Heritage Site. Small trees are growing on the roof of the building in the background. It is a part of the site management plan to remove growth from the roofs every three years. The removal is necessary for the long-term protection of the roof timber structure and tile roofing. The roof in this picture had been cleaned one year previously

tics, or defects in timber, are related to grain direction, reaction wood, knots, longitudinal separations (such as shakes) and pitch pockets. In addition to these growth characteristics, which may reduce the strength of wood, defects in wood may also occur as a result of poor seasoning: timber may warp or checks and splits may develop. To prevent splitting from occurring during air drying, the end grains of individual boards or timbers can be protected either by cleats, preferably of metal, fixed to their ends, or, more commonly, by the application of a water-proof seal. The function of an end seal is to maintain a higher moisture content under the seal than compared to unsealed end grains. Waxes of various kinds have often proved to be beneficial.

7.7 Maintenance

The best way of ensuring the continued preservation of a building is to carry out regular maintenance. Monitoring and maintenance are covered by Article 3 of the Wood Committee's Principles, which recommends that a coherent strategy of regular monitoring and maintenance should be established because this is crucial for the protection of historic timber structures and their cultural significance. By maintenance we mean taking actions to keep the timber structure operational or to sustain it in its existing state. The objective of a maintenance policy should be to retain the structure in an optimum state, at as a low cost as is feasible. Unfortunately, many owners of historic buildings take a

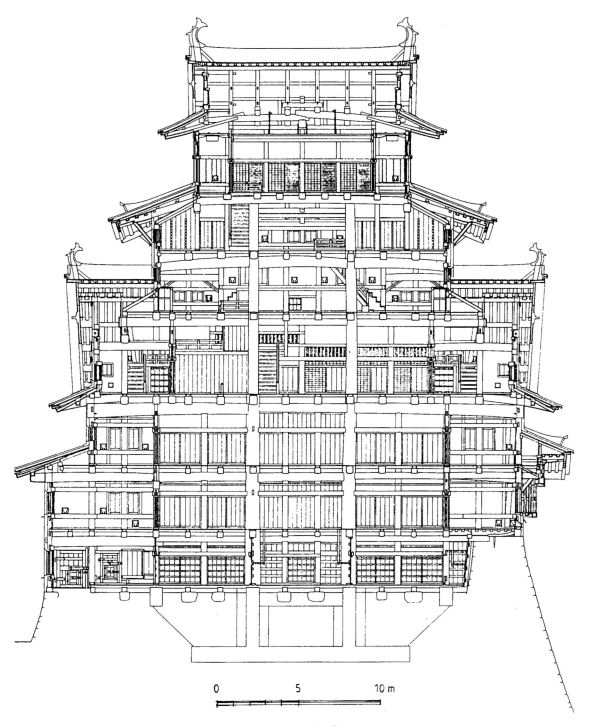

0   5   10 m

Figure 7.12 Himeji Castle, Japan, a World Heritage Site, built in the early seventeenth century. Section. This is a timber structure with external plastering. (Drawing from *Kokuho Himeji-jo hozon shuri koji hokokusho*, volume 6: *Tenshu*. Agency for Cultural Affairs, Japan, 1965)

negative approach to the principle of regular maintenance and problems are dealt with only as they occur. However, prevention is better than cure, and it is also less expensive. For instance, an outbreak of dry rot may be caused by a single leaking gutter or downpipe over a long period of time. A problem like this can be remedied at a small fraction of the cost necessary to deal with dry rot. Therefore, neglect of such routine small repairs inevitably leads to greater efforts and expense and ultimately to major repairs, which might have been avoided or at least postponed.

Maintenance of buildings is generally regarded as a continuous process to prevent the decay of the materials and the deterioration of the structure, such as regular repainting and removal of leaves from gutters. When buildings are regularly maintained, the period between more drastic interventions can be greatly prolonged. For instance, in Japan, at Himeji Castle, built at the beginning of the seventeenth century, the castle lords checked vertical and horizontal distortions every twenty to thirty years, and reinforced or repaired the buildings as required, by adding braces and supports, and replacing roof tiles. This was regarded as regular maintenance (Larsen, 1994: 5).

Regular inspections are a vital part of the procedure for building maintenance, and for the monitoring of the development of a structure. A systematic approach using a manual for guidance will help in planning the time scale and scope of inspections. The interval between inspections may be governed by local needs and uses of the building, and the environmental conditions. Records of all inspections should be kept. The inspection should be carried out by a professional, such as an architectural conservator or a master-builder, who is able to draw up a report containing recommendations.

Maintenance work can be divided into two main categories: routine or day-to-day

Figure 7.13 Grass growing along wooden walls accumulates moisture and leads to decay

maintenance, and periodic maintenance (Mills, 1994). The first depends on the constant vigilance of the building owner. It includes actions that can usually be dealt with without the need to employ outside labour. On the other hand, periodic maintenance is more in the nature of minor repairs and therefore requires the assistance of a professional craftsman, preferably with a knowledge of historic timber structures. Day-to-day maintenance includes actions such as clearing leaves and accumulated silt from gutters, controlling plant growth, checking faults in rainwater receptacles, removing bird droppings and checking ventilation. Minor repairs and maintenance involving professional assistance include maintenance of eaves, gutters and downpipes, repair to metal coverings, adjustment of roof covering such as slates and roof tiles, and repainting. In both categories the main issue to remember is that prevention is best achieved by ensuring that the timber is kept dry and well ventilated (Brereton, 1995: 7).

7.8 Fire and fire protection

Timber structures are particularly vulnerable to fire. Therefore, fire protection is essential in a comprehensive preventive conservation strategy for timber structures. Under the influence of sufficiently strong heat sources, wood decomposes to a mixture of volatile substances, tars and highly reactive carbonaceous char. Gas-phase oxidation of the combustible volatile substances and tarry products produces flaming combustion. The vapours and gases burn when mixed with the oxygen in the air and the reaction becomes exothermic: the heat that is released promotes continued combustion or pyrolysis. The most commonly quoted ignition temperature for wood is 250 degrees centigrade, when volatilisation of cell wall polymers occurs. In general, low density species ignite at lower temperatures than those of high density. As a consequence, decayed wood with a lower density than normal ignites at a lower temperature.

The size of timber is of great importance in relation to combustion. Heat must be transferred from the surface to the inner portion of a piece if wood is to burn. As wood is a good heat insulating material, conduction of heat through the material is poor or slow. The layer of charcoal formed during combustion also helps to protect the unburned wood below it, and the penetration of the member by fire is retarded. It takes about 5–6 hours before timber of pine (*Pinus sylvestris*) with a thickness of 16–18 cm is completely charred. Fire-retardant paints have no tradition in historic timber structures and should, if possible, be avoided.

Fire precaution legislation as applied to all existing buildings is concerned with human fire safety. The preservation of the fabric of a building, prevention of damage to its aesthetic features and protection of its contents from loss by fire are areas that are not covered by legislation. Moreover, the fire protection of historic buildings and sites is more complex than the protection of ordinary contemporary buildings because of technical problems, alarm problems, problems related to secondary damage, aesthetic problems, economic problems, and the like. Historic buildings also pose a particular risk in relation to fires due to their building materials, construction techniques, their use and, often, the sites where they are located (Larsen and Marstein, 1992).

The first step in a fire protection programme should be an assessment of the fire risks in order to obtain the most appropriate fire protection at the lowest cost. The fire protection programme will inevitably be restricted by such factors as economic and technological constraints. However, this is not to say that low-tech solutions, based on simple fire-fighting devices such as fire hoses and hand-held fire extinguishers, must necessarily be inferior to a fire protection strategy based on sophisticated automatic alarm systems with a direct alarm link to the fire-brigade and expensive and comprehensive automatic fire extinguishing systems such as sprinklers. Concerning the latter, we must also take into consideration the fact that, in addition to the expense of installing such systems, they are also costly and often

Figure 7.14 Fire protection equipment at a Norwegian farm where there are a number of listed buildings. The owner has created a small pond to provide water for the fire-fighting equipment

complex to maintain. Sprinklers, moreover, may cause much damage if they are activated in a false alarm. An additional problem with electronic alarm and sprinkler systems is that the alarms and sprinkler heads and the necessary electrical cables and water pipes often may be difficult to adapt to the sensitive interior of historic buildings (Marstein, 1992). Article 13 of the Wood Committee's Principles recommends that fire detection and prevention systems should be installed with due recognition of the historic and aesthetic significance of the structure or site.

Fire extinguishing systems are almost entirely dependent on water, and their installation involves great expense. When cultural properties are located in remote areas where it is impossible to use the public water supply, huge water tanks have to be constructed. The network of pipes from the water tanks, or for that matter from the public supply, necessitates careful planning in order to avoid disturbance of archaeological material in the ground.

7.8.1 Cultural heritage – a real challenge for fire protection

Fire protection of historic buildings differs from other forms of fire protection in one significant aspect: the principal concern is the safeguarding of the building, not people. However, these two different starting points do not produce significantly different results. In most cases, good fire protection of a building will also protect people. The major difference lies in the emphasis on escape routes.

Safeguarding protected structures from fire involves a strengthening of the requirements laid down for other forms of fire protection. A best possible cost/usage effect is always desirable. Within the field of listed buildings, this is particularly important. Clearly, costs and resources are inter-connected, but in this instance, a greater understanding and greater emphasis on costs is required. Costs in this connection are more to do with incursions than money. We understand incursions as:

- physical destruction, e.g. drilling holes
- long term physical damage due to poor solutions which result in condensation, water ingress etc.
- physical wear and tear through operation and maintenance, repair etc.
- water damage resulting from accidental activation of extinguishing equipment
- water damage resulting from extinguishing a fire

Figure 7.15   Demonstrating the use of a water gun in Tsumago town, Nagano, Japan. Tsumago is an historic postal town designated as a preservation district

- actions which have a negative effect on the whole aesthetic experience
- destruction of possible archaeological remains, e.g. through the installation of a water supply.

In a normal building, most of this would not apply, but if a building is to be maintained in an 'eternity perspective', then it is quite different. The lifetime for electronic equipment in exposed environments is between 5 and 10 years, which means that the incursions resulting from installation and maintenance will be very large after only a few decades. In order to experience the atmosphere in an 800-year-old stave church, for example, all the fire protection equipment should be hidden from view. Accidental activation of a water-based

extinguishing system can wash away decorative paintings, which may be of significant value in a global context. Thus the challenges raised by such incursions are formidable. None the less, the safety requirement is huge, because this material cultural inheritance represents non-renewable assets. A building which is gone is lost forever, no matter how many good copies may be made. Optimal safety and minimal incursions are therefore important and meaningful goals.

7.8.2 Safety strategies

It is important that everything that is carried out is thought through first. We therefore need a safety strategy.

1. *Causes of fire:* After going through possible causes of fire, the most obvious causes must be selected and weighed up against what is feasible historically, practically, technically and financially, and the limitations in these areas.
2. *Fire prevention measures:* These are measures directed at probable causes of fire in order to prevent fire from breaking out. These measures are implemented by comparing possible causes of fire with what is technically and practically feasible, within financial and historic frameworks.
3. *Residual risk:* This deals with failure of fire prevention measures and fires that result from causes not covered by such measures. This residual risk is usually greater than is acceptable.
4. *Fire limitation measures:* These measures are directed at reducing the damage following a fire or the extent of a fire. The residual risk is weighed up against the possible course of the fire and what is practically and technically possible within financial and historic frameworks.
5. *Accepted residual risk:* Within the residual risk, which we have to accept, lies failure of fire prevention measures or fires that result from causes not covered by such measures, while *simultaneously* there is a failure in, or under-dimensioning of, fire limitation measures. The accepted residual risk should be inversely proportional to the historic value.

This strategy clearly distinguishes between fire prevention measures and fire limitation measures. Fire *prevention* measures are measures that are directed at the cause of a fire. Examples are:

- lightning protection equipment to prevent fire should the structure be struck by lightning

- cleaning, locking burglar alarms, and, in extreme cases, video surveillance to prevent arson
- working conditions which everyone who works on a building must sign to prevent fire resulting from the work they are carrying out
- critical appraisal and upgrading of electrical equipment to prevent fire resulting from failure in the electrical system
- evaluation of the need for installations and usage patterns to exclude as many causes of fire as possible etc.

Fire *limitation* measures include automatic extinguishing equipment and in some cases dividing up the building to prevent the spread of fire (compartmentalisation). Alarm systems have no value in themselves for building safety, but must be taken into account when considering installations. Such installations may include accessible extinguishing equipment, ideally fire hoses combined with adjacent equipment. In ideal situations, the fire service will be based near enough for this to be significant in evaluating building safety.

The division between fire prevention measures and fire limitation measures reflects an acceptance that it is far better to avoid a fire than to put one out, however quickly this is done. For protected buildings which cannot be replaced, avoiding fires altogether is of the utmost priority. Such an attitude does not necessarily imply mistrust of automatic extinguishers or of the fire brigade, but a clear understanding of the scope of the damage following a fire, not least damage caused in extinguishing the fire.

7.8.3 Simple logic and logical simplicity

Safety strategies should involve simple logic. However, it is not always easy to find

Figure 7.16   Borgund stave church, Sogn, Norway, during a sprinkler fire extinguishing system test in 1982. All the 28 medieval stave churches have fire detection and fire extinguishing systems. Traditional sprinkler systems and advanced mist systems are used

solutions that involve logical simplicity. It is important to avoid connecting different elements which have differing functions. Extinguishers that are activated upon smoke detection are still being designed. If the detection system detects smoke, the extinguishing system will put out the fire. However, failure in one system will have a domino effect and there is also the risk that the extinguishers will not be activated in the event of fire as a result of lightning. In every situation where lightning is a possible cause of fire, it is totally inappropriate to have an electronically or electrically operated extinguishing system. Autonomous extinguishers, that is, smaller units which can be put into buildings and operated independently of the electricity supply, water or other external support, are being developed. Examples of such extinguishers are inert aerosols, sprinklers or water mist. Water mist extinguishers, where the extinguishing agent is used in such small quantities that it does not damage the building or the interior, are now coming onto the market.

It is important that operation and maintenance routines are developed for safety equipment. These should be based on local routine inspections and systematic external inspections of the whole safety installation. That is to say, there should be one single address for responsibility for safety, not division of responsibility for the individual elements or technical installations. This is because it is not an individual installation which matters, but safety in itself. An alarm system has no value if the alarm does not provoke a reaction.

Electronics are sensitive and often develop faults. However, within the field of smoke detection, aspiration detection can be used in hostile environments. A warning system can be constructed with three elements: the detector unit, central unit and telephone connection to the fire service. Each of these elements is itself very complicated. It is therefore important to choose solutions which are as simple and robust as possible. Simple alarm systems are preferable to complicated ones, since an alarm signal is essentially as simple as *on* or *off*, *smoke* or *no smoke*.

Logical simplicity also includes the right level of safety or the right degree of safety. A building can never be 100 per cent secure, to the extent that the residual risk is 0 per cent. The residual risk will always be there, and the closer one gets to 100 per cent safety, the more expensive each improvement will be. The big leap from no safety to good levels of safety lies in cheap and simple measures. In a building with limited use it is both cheaper and more effective to install circuit breakers than to install an alarm system. Working instructions for workmen re-roofing a building can reduce the risk significantly more than round-the-clock surveillance. A critical evaluation of use and storage on a farm, for example, leading to the installation of a simple alarm system and two powerful fire hoses in the farmyard, will mean that 60–70 per cent of the achievable level of safety has already been achieved. To reach a higher level of safety, costly measures such as sprinkler systems may be required.

We feel that the most important element in the fire protection strategy is making the public – including the custodians of cultural properties – aware that fire is always an imminent threat to cultural properties made of wood. The experience of the Japanese following a fire in the world's oldest timber structure, the Golden Hall of the Horyu-ji temple in 1949, is particularly useful as an example of how a catastrophe may be turned into something positive for the future (Larsen, 1994: 58–61). The fire had a tremendous impact, not only on the question of fire protection of historic buildings in Japan, but also on protection of cultural properties in general. In 1955, the year after the rebuilding of the hall had been completed, the Japanese Agency for Cultural Affairs declared 26 January, the day the fire occurred, as 'Cultural Properties Fire Prevention Day'. On this day each year fire-fighting drills and other related activities are organised with the co-operation of the Fire Defence Agency and the local fire brigades on the sites of cultural properties. Reports of these activities are widely publicised, and the public at large becomes aware of the necessity of fire protection of historic buildings. Measures such as these raise the awareness of the public, and are probably the most important steps in a comprehensive fire protection strategy.

8

Like seasoned timber, never gives: the durability of wood as a building material

All properties of timber as an elegant and versatile structural material originate in the chemical, cell wall and cellular structures of wood. However, the main disadvantage of wood – its susceptibility to decay – is also a feature of that same composition and structure. The main factors and agencies, some of them interdependent, causing deterioration or destruction of wood are attacks by wood-rotting fungi, wood-boring animals and bacteria, mechanical wear, chemicals, weathering, heat and fire.

No timber is immune to deterioration if exposed to the natural environment for a sufficiently long period. However, the service life of individual pieces varies considerably and may well be more than a thousand years. This depends on factors such as the species of wood concerned, the amount of sapwood present in the actual piece, the use to which the timber is put and the situations and environmental conditions to which it is exposed. Under certain conditions, wood will outlast almost any other conventional structural material (Borgin, 1971).

8.1 Heartwood: natural durability and stability

Knowledge of the natural durability of wood was central to traditional understanding of the quality of building materials. The use of naturally durable wood, together with

adequate and proper detailing, resulted in buildings that have lasted for centuries.

Natural durability of wood is the inherent resistance of wood to decay caused by wood-destroying organisms. In practice, it is the heartwood that contains the chemicals (extractives) which have a toxic effect on wood-destroying organisms. The properties resulting from the presence of extractives in wood have been recognised for a long time. With the development of cutting tools, logs could be cut for construction and other purposes, and knowledge of the advantages of heartwood accumulated, particularly with regard to appearance and durability. The old master-builders knew which species of wood were suitable for different building purposes, and which parts of the tree they should use.

Of particular interest for us today is the widespread use of heartwood for construction purposes in external building elements in historic timber structures. In Norway, the survival of some 250 medieval timber buildings is attributed to the use of pine heartwood (*Pinus sylvestris*) in the original construction work. In well-built houses, pine heartwood was used almost exclusively for all external building elements.

However, exploitation of the natural durability of wood is universal. In the tenth century BC, the export of cedar wood from Lebanon (*Cedrus libani*) to Jerusalem for building the temple of Solomon was doubtless due not only to the size and medium density of the cedar logs, but also to their durability. Teak (*Tectona grandis*) was exported some 4000 years BC from India to Babylon and Yemen where, it would seem, its durability was recognised. The Romans removed the non-durable sapwood from oak (*Quercus robur*), pine and cypress when those woods were used for buildings (Hillis, 1987: 1–2; 58–59). In China, it was obviously well known that certain species had properties that made them more suitable for use in different parts of the structures. Careful selection of different kinds of timber for different uses can be seen in the Imperial Palace in Beijing. The Chinese of Guangdong and Yunnan provinces used only heartwood in their buildings (Zhong and Chen, 1986: 303–304). Teak has long been valued for its very high resistance to fungal decay and insect and borer attacks, and for its dimensional stability after drying. It was widely used for house building in South East Asia and Malaysia.

We have come to see the use of naturally durable wood in traditional building techniques as a sustainable method that we could well study, revive and adopt, wherever possible, in current construction work. This kind of knowledge seems almost to have been forgotten today by modern wood scientists when they evaluate the natural durability of wood species. In a world of diminishing resources, there is a growing need for the development of renewable resources, such as heartwood from durable species of wood. The provision and use of renewable resources such as this can be increased by research and understanding.

8.2 Heartwood formation

Wood tissue is made up of four major chemical constituents: cellulose (45–50%), hemicel-luloses (20–25%), lignin (20–30%) and extractives (0–10%). The numbers in parentheses broadly indicate the average contents of the dry weight of the constituents of normal wood tissue. The term *extractive* includes a wide range of chemical types and a very large number of individual compounds which can be extracted from wood or bark with polar or non-polar solvents. Usually, extractives are considered to be those compounds that are soluble in organic solvents. Extractives include such chemical substances as terpenoids, fatty acids and phenolic compounds. The composition of the extractives in the different zones of the same tree may differ, and even the extractives in different tissues in those zones may differ (Hillis, 1987: 96). Studies have also shown an increase in extractives content from the pith to the periphery of the heartwood and from the top to the butt log.

These organic crystals, or extractives, have toxic or repellent effects on organisms that attack wood. Therefore, although the extractives constitute a relatively minor part of the mass of dry wood, they may have a significant effect on the use of the wood for structural or other purposes.

Wood scientists recognised the role of wood extractives in decay resistance as early as 1924 (Weiss and Gale, 1983). Research has shown that the amount of extractives is genetically dependent to a certain extent. Consequently, it should be possible to improve the natural decay resistance of trees through plant breeding. It is assumed that the relative contents of heartwood decreases with increasing growth speed. Because the extractives are associated with the heartwood, the amount can also be influenced through forest management..

In saplings (very young trees), the entire wood portion of the trunk is involved in the upward conduction of sap, that is, water and nutrients absorbed by the roots from the soil.

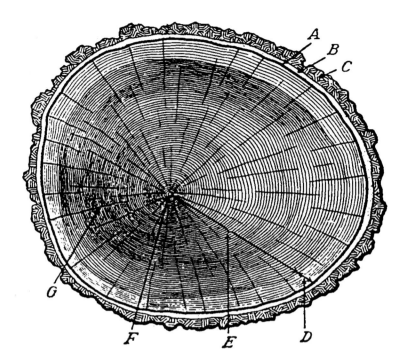

Figure 8.1 Section of a tree: A, cambium; B, inner bark (phloem); C, outer bark; D, sapwood; E, heartwood; F, pith; G, rays

This wood is called sapwood. The new wood cells formed in the cambium function initially as sapwood. The main role of the sapwood, the most recently formed wood, is that of conduction.

As the tree matures and the trunk increases in girth, it no longer needs the entire cross-section for the conduction of sap. In the central area, the cells cease to function in their conductive role and serve mainly in the mechanical support of the tree. Moreover, the food-storing cells die. The secretion of extractives accompanies the death of these cells. This part of the wood (*xylem*) is termed heartwood. Thus, heartwood is defined as the inner layers of the wood in the growing tree which have ceased to contain living cells, and in which the reserve material (e.g. starch) has been removed or converted into heartwood substance (Hillis, 1987: 21). The heartwood portion enlarges with time. As new wood, which is sapwood, is formed in the cambium,

additional interior sapwood adjacent to the heartwood zone is converted to heartwood. Some species are composed entirely of heartwood with only a narrow band of sapwood (e.g. larch), whereas others possess only a small amount of heartwood.

However, heartwood formation is complex and there is no single satisfactory explanation. An interdisciplinary approach in this field is necessary since chemical studies alone will not provide the answer to heartwood formation and neither will anatomical, cytological or other studies (Hillis, 1987: VI).

Wound wood forms in response to mechanical or microbiological damage. The formation of wound wood is related to a dynamic mechanism in the host to minimise further damage. In mechanically wounded wood, researchers have observed the same types of chemical compounds as in heartwood. They have used various terms to describe this process, such as 'pathological heartwood' and 'discoloured wood' (Hillis, 1987: 157).

In Scandinavia, from the Middle Ages until the first half of the twentieth century, two techniques were used to increase the section of heartwood in standing pines by wounding the tree before felling. One method was to cut off strips of bark, thus destroying the inner bark, which gradually reduced the tree's ability to transport nutrients downwards. The growth process was halted and the need to transport water and nutrients (sap) upwards through the stem was reduced, and a larger section of the sapwood converted to heartwood. By strip-barking over a period of two to three years, most of the cross-section of the tree was converted to heartwood. Another method was to halt the growth of the tree by cutting off the top, leaving only a few branches. This reduced the need for transport of sap, and the greater part of the sapwood was thus converted to heartwood. After four to six years, the heartwood covered almost the complete cross-section of the trunk.

Traditional practices, such as the 'artificial' formation of heartwood by wounding the tree, are only rarely verified by scientific evidence. However, research is currently being carried out in Norway, Sweden and Finland into the formation and properties of pathological heartwood. In addition, research is also going on concerning the influence of forestry aspects and practices on the formation of heartwood. If the controlling factors for heartwood formation can be predicted and a relationship found, then this would help in selecting the most suitable group of trees for a particular purpose, as well as in the choice of the most suitable silvicultural practices (Hillis, 1987: 69). Various attempts have been made to relate growth rate to the proportion of heartwood or sapwood in a tree by means of the size of the crown. However, no exact correlation has been established. There are also contradictory conclusions on the influence of the environment, for example concerning the level of humidity and availability of water (Hillis, 1987: 69–71).

8.3 Heartwood characteristics

Heartwood has a number of characteristics that distinguish it from sapwood (Parham and Gray, 1984: 42–45):

1. The entire region is normally infiltrated and encrusted with organic extractives derived from the parenchyma (food-storing) cells. The extractives in many species have toxic effects on fungi, insects and marine borers and thus function as natural preservatives when wood is used for structural purposes.

Figure 8.2 The end section of a larch log (*Larix decidua*). The heartwood covers almost the whole cross-section; there is only a narrow outer ring of sapwood

2. The moisture content of heartwood is reduced to a level much lower than that of sapwood. This is caused by pit aspiration in softwoods and the formation of tyloses in hardwoods.
3. Heartwood may take on a distinct colour and may be darker than the sapwood (for example, in pines, larches and oaks). In other species (for example, spruce and aspen) there is no noticeable change in colour, but the heartwood still has a high extractives content as well as exhibiting the physical alterations described above.

Because of the favourable properties of heartwood, sapwood was normally cut off before timber was used for structural purposes. This goes a long way towards explaining the long durability of many historic structures all over the world. However, as far as mechanical properties are concerned, there is no difference between sapwood and heartwood.

In the terms of wood science, natural durability is defined as the inherent resistance of wood to attack by wood-destroying organisms. The term *treatability* refers to the ease with which wood can be penetrated by a liquid, such as a wood preservative (European Standard EN 350-2). The ability of wood to absorb moisture has an important effect upon its service life in buildings. The service life of wood in buildings, provided the wood is not in contact with the ground, depends on both its durability and its treatability. A wood of a given durability which has low moisture-absorbing characteristics will, due to its reduced water uptake, generally last markedly longer than a wood of the same durability rating, but which is more absorbent.

Softwoods consist primarily of longitudinal tracheids, vertically oriented along the trunk axis. The longitudinal tracheids have closed ends, but a special cell wall feature – a small opening or recess known as a pit – allows movement of the tree's sap stream from one tracheid to another. A pit in one cell occurs opposite a pit in an adjacent cell, forming a pit pair. When wood dries, substantial capillary and surface tension forces develop as water retreats from the cell lumen through the pits. When this happens, the pit membranes move to one side and effectively seal one of the apertures. This condition, known as pit aspiration, greatly impedes the subsequent movement of fluids or gases through the wood tissue. Pit aspiration occurs naturally in softwoods upon conversion of sapwood to heartwood.

In hardwoods, the vertical transport of sap is performed by vessel elements. A vessel consists of individual vessel elements stacked one on top of the other in the longitudinal direction of the stem. In many species, when the lumens of vessels become filled with air as sapwood is converted to heartwood, living parenchyma cells form outgrowths through the pit cavities into the lumens of vessels. These outgrowths of parenchyma cell walls are termed tyloses. When a considerable number of tyloses have been formed, the permeability of the wood is reduced as the vessel lumens become completely blocked.

8.4 The natural durability of solid wood from the perspective of wood science

Natural decay resistance or naturally durable wood is a concept with varying meaning. In the 'scientific' sense, this is expressed in standards such as the European EN350-2, where the durability of the wood against fungal decay is calculated on the basis of an experiment that is of little relevance to the use of wood in timber structures. In this experiment, heartwood stakes are half-buried out of doors in soil and the time it takes before the stake rots is noted.

Figure 8.3   Shakespeare's Globe, London, UK (1997). Oak heartwood (*Quercus robur*) was used in all external (exposed) members, although the architect and builder Peter McCurdy reckoned that the original structure probably contained timber with a high proportion of sapwood

This resembles the way in which the medieval Norwegian stave churches were built in the eleventh century, with posts set in holes in the soil, a building technique which was universal in ancient times. The builders dug a hole in the ground, inserted a post and filled in around the post with pebbles and stones in order to keep the post erect. Research has suggested that the stave churches with posts in holes in the ground probably stood for 100–150 years before the wood in contact with the ground rotted, and the structure became unstable or collapsed. The posts were probably made of pine (*Pinus sylvestris*).

During the twelfth century a fundamental innovation took place in stave church construction technology. The structure was literally lifted out of the ground and placed on raft and sill beams upon a stone foundation. The construction material was still pine wood, ideally heartwood. We can conclude that this innovation extended the life of such timber structures by 700–800 years, judging from the existing stave churches. In addition, more than 250 log buildings from the Middle Ages are still to be found in Norway today. These timber structures are between 400 and 700 years old and are all built of pine, mostly heartwood.

The European standard EN 350-2 concerning the natural durability of wood classifies the natural durability to wood-destroying fungi according to a five-class system from

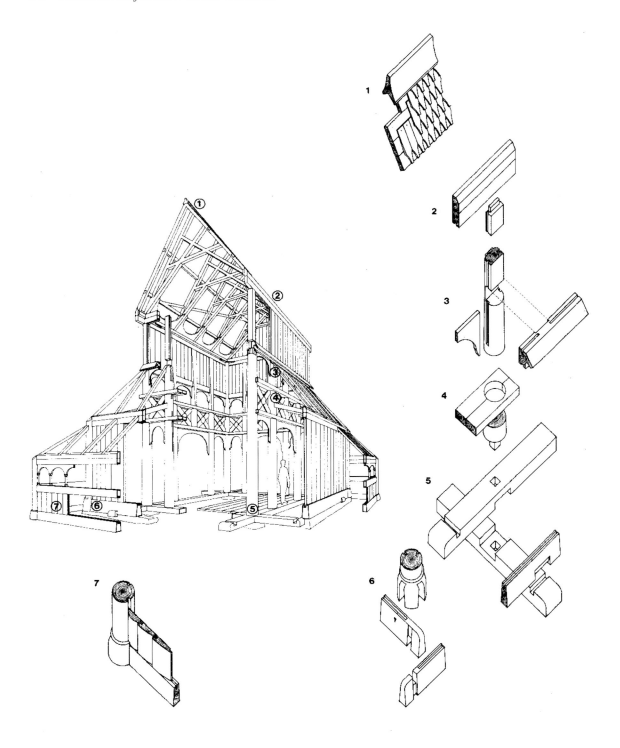

Figure 8.4   Norwegian medieval stave church construction

Figure 8.5 External boarding of aspen (*Populus tremula*), about 80 years old. This external boarding has never been treated with paint or coating. It is still in excellent condition, despite being in an exposed situation

'very durable' (class 1) to 'not durable' (class 5). For example, larch (*Larix decidua*) and Scots pine (*Pinus sylvestris*) have similar characteristics: the natural durability against wood-destroying fungi is classified as moderate to slight (classes 3–4). Both species are susceptible to insect decay. Larch is classified as extremely difficult to treat, while pine is difficult to extremely difficult. Both species have narrow sap-width. European oak (*Quercus robur*) shares many characteristics with these two softwoods. It is, however, more resistant to fungal decay (and therefore classified as durable) and also to insect decay.

When we think of the large number of timber structures made of pine (*Pinus sylvestris*), dating back several hundred years,

still standing in Scandinavia, it hardly seems relevant to characterise this species as being moderately to slightly durable in relation to fungal decay. This classification is, of course, correct if we sink the wood down into the soil. If pine heartwood is used sensibly, however, like the old master-builders did, the durability will improve greatly. Another example from Norway which is contrary to the wood scientist's definition of durability is aspen (*Populus tremula*). The natural durability of aspen is characterised as poor. Nonetheless, aspen wood was extensively used in Norwegian timber structures in olden times, particularly for weather-boarding on barns. People knew that it was not necessary to treat aspen boards that were used as weatherboarding and yet they still lasted for at least

100 years. Along the Norwegian coast, people knew that quay pillars made from aspen were superior due to the wood's resistance to certain marine borers. Yet this is a wood evaluated by modern wood science as being poor in durability.

We may conclude that old wooden buildings form part of a huge knowledge bank for the understanding of wood properties. We would like to believe the situation is similar in most countries – the reason why old timber structures exist is that previous generations of master-carpenters understood the properties of wood and how to use wood correctly. The assets in these 'knowledge banks' are so huge that they contradict many of the theories of modern wood science. What is the point of putting a stake into the earth to see how fast it rots? In the old days, no one in Norway would have considered using pine, or the heartwood of pine for that matter, for fence poles, for instance. There were other, better-suited wood species, such as juniper (*Juniperus communis*) or oak (*Quercus robur*) which could be used for such purposes.

In the first century BC, Vitruvius proposed in his treatise *De architectura* that architecture was characterised by the fulfilling of three criteria, those of *firmitas* (durability), *utilitas* (convenience) and *venustas* (beauty). The classical ideals of architecture have, from time to time, been revived in periods of neo-classicism in European architectural history, thus reminding people of the existence of universal architectural values. However, the theory of functionalism in the late 1920s and early 1930s represented a fundamental break with the classical theory by claiming that architecture consisted in the balancing of form, function and technology. Thus, by making form the first and pre-eminent criterion, the relationship between the characterising concepts of architecture was turned upside down. According to the classical

ideals of architecture, technology was the most important issue. Only by building durably by using the right material in the right place was the builder able to build houses that were beautiful as well. By focusing on form as the most important factor, we have come to forget this universal truth. If we look at our historic buildings, we will see buildings that retain their technical soundness, have aged with dignity, and still appeal to us aesthetically centuries after they were built.

However, to make tradition-based knowledge work, research is required in order to verify traditional practices within a scientific context. It is also necessary to demonstrate through examples how the various traditional technologies and use of wood can be applied within a modern architectural context. It is important to have examples in order to broaden the interest and understanding among contemporary architects so that they see the benefits of the tradition-based knowledge of wood.

At the same time, we must also acknowledge that in traditional building technology it was the interaction of several factors that resulted in durable buildings. One example of this was the use of durable wood in exposed building elements. However, this is not in itself sufficient to make a building or building part durable. In Norway, for example, the master-builders also required timber to be sawn in special ways in order to increase durability. In historic timber structures in Norway, we have observed that radially sawn wood was used for structural timbers that were exposed to the elements.

8.5 Cutting patterns and durability

The most straightforward method of conversion by sawing is the 'through and through' method, where the log is sawn using a succession of cuts. Boards from the central part are radially sawn, the remainder tangentially. For timber from the temperate zone with prominent annual rings, the way of sawing is extremely important, the crucial part being the position of the annual rings relative to the wide face of the piece in question. Shrinkage, warping, abrasion resistance, ease of painting and appearance are all properties that differ according to the position of the annual rings on the cross-section.

The sawing of a log so that the wide face of a board is almost parallel to the annual rings (tangential sawing) is known as slash cutting for softwoods (also known as flat grain) and plain sawn for hardwoods. Sawing so that the annual rings are almost perpendicular to the wide face of the board (radial sawing) is known as rift cut for softwoods (also known as vertical or edge grain) and quarter sawn for hardwoods. Between these two extremes there are many intermediate pieces. Pieces where the annual rings cross at about 45 degrees are known as bastard cut.

As the wood dries, it shrinks. Shrinkage in the tangential direction is greater than in any other direction. Consequently, in a slash cut (plain sawn) piece of timber with its broad face nearly parallel to the annual rings, the length along the trace of an annual ring shortens, and the piece warps appreciably with its convex side against the centre of the log. The rift cut (or quarter sawn) piece shows such distortion only on its narrow edges. Although its dimension is slightly reduced due to radial shrinkage, the piece remains flat over its wider dimension. The bastard cut piece, if it has been square in cross-section when sawn, deforms during drying to become diamond-shaped.

Rift cut (quarter sawn) timber is obviously superior to slash cut (plain sawn). Technically, it is possible to convert a log so

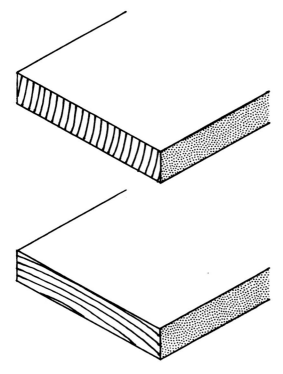

Figure 8.6 Radial (*upper*) and tangential sawing

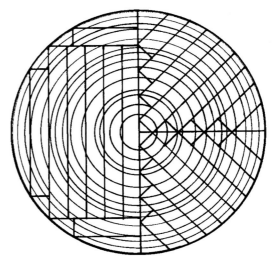

Figure 8.7 Two different sawing patterns: rift cut (*right*) and slash cut (*left*)

as to produce true radially sawn boards only. However, sawing to produce a higher percentage of such pieces would require turning the log more frequently. It is, therefore, not feasible in commercially operated sawmills. Rift cutting or quarter sawing dates back to a period when labour was relatively cheap. It is therefore unlikely that the architectural conservator or craftsman will find radially sawn timber of the required dimensions and quantities in the timberyard.

As radially sawn timber expands and contracts less than timber sawn tangentially during variations in humidity, it will be less likely to crack. This minimises the possibility of attack by fungi and insects, which tend to enter wood through cracks. Thus, proper cutting patterns help to prolong the life of the timber. Furthermore, the building parts in wood should be assembled and detailed in a way that promotes long life. The interplay between the right material treated in the right way and used correctly, resulted in durable buildings. This is the lesson we need to relearn and re-introduce into contemporary architecture.

8.6 What happens when wood ages: wood durability

Alterations to the composition of the wood begin shortly after a tree has been felled. Chemical and structural variations in wood are caused by several factors. These include reduction in the water content, the access of oxygen, the residual activity of the enzymes present in wood and the settlement of micro-organisms. Moreover, in this process we must also consider the influence of a number of environmental factors such as visible and ultraviolet light, heat and frost, ozone and atmospheric oxygen, and the erosive effects of wind, rain, snow, hail and other airborne particles, damp and fluctuations in humidity,

loads and variations in loads. However, seen over time, these variations are actually very slow.

Studies of spruce wood and pine wood from timber samples respectively 290 and 365 years old showed no variations in the microstructure of the cell walls which can be attributed to ageing. An insignificant reduction of 2–3 per cent in the cellulose and lignin contents was found in a study of teak wood from a 1,800 year old Buddhist temple in India (Fengel, 1991: 156). In the late 1960s, relatively well-preserved wood samples between 500 and 2000 years old were found in India, and woodcarvings from Maya temples were found in the termite-ridden jungles of Central America at the same time. Tests with termites and fungi using these ancient samples and their isolated extractives proved that the compounds had retained their effectiveness (Fengel, 1991: 165).

However, although people have used wood for many thousands of years, there is still a great deal that wood researchers do not understand about the properties of the material. For example, it is uncertain if and how the structure of wood and the behaviour of wood under loads changes with ageing. The results of the few studies that have been made on small, so-called 'clear specimens' (specimens with straight grain and without defects) have not produced any definitive conclusions (Sandin, 1996: 55). A recent European study concluded that in the absence of decay, it is impossible to determine an 'age effect' on wood from test data. The test data were obtained from small clear wood specimens extracted from old sound timber members and tested to failure point (bending, compression, impact etc.). The tests showed no significant differences in strength and stiffness values compared with new material (Bonamini, 1995: D3/3).

This conclusion contradicts observations made by Professor Jiro Kohara in Japan over

Figure 8.8 Detail of the sill beam in a Norwegian log structure from the late eighteenth century. Note the extremely narrow width of the annual rings, and that the sapwood content is insignificant. It is very well preserved, despite exposure to the elements over two centuries

increased remarkably between zero and 300 years and remained fairly constant after that, for as long as 1300 years. Shear strength remained nearly constant for 900 years but decreased slightly after that. While static bending increased somewhat between zero and 300 years and remained fairly constant thereafter, impact bending decreased until the wood was about 600 years old and then remained constant. Due to the lack of studies of wood as old as the Japanese specimens, we must conclude for the time being that there are no general rules on how the properties of wood change with ageing.

8.7 Weathering of wood

In outdoor environments, wooden surfaces undergo a series of changes caused mainly by a combination of solar radiation and moisture. These changes are covered by the term 'weathering'. As a result of weathering, wood loses its surface coherence as the strength of cell wall bonds is lost near the surface. Surfaces become rough as the grain raises, the wood checks and the checks may develop into cracks. Furthermore, the grain may loosen and boards may warp and twist and pull away from fasteners. The roughened surface changes colour and gathers dirt. Weathering is not the same as decay, but the defects caused by weathering may provide conditions conducive to decay as the checks and raised grain facilitate the entrance into the wood of fungal spores and insects (Feist and Hon, 1984; Kaila, 1987a).

As weathering continues, rainwater washes out degraded portions and further erosion takes place. The rate of erosion depends on a number of factors. In general, the denser the wood, the less erosion there is. Thus, earlywood erodes more quickly than latewood. Reported erosion rates vary between 1 mm per century to 13 mm per century. In Japan it

fifty years ago and published in the early 1950s as a series of articles on the permanence of wood. One of the studies was on the change of the mechanical properties of old timber (Kohara, 1954). Professor Kohara studied the durability of specimens of Japanese cypress (*Chamaecyparis obtusa*). The nine specimens he studied were between 359 and 1,300 years old. He compared these old pieces with pieces of new wood and found that the compression strength

Figure 8.9 Detail from a log structure from the Todai-ji temple in Nara, Japan, built in the eighth century (see Figure 3.8). The cross-section of the original eighth-century logs has been greatly reduced due to weathering. The new log, clearly distinguishable, was added during repair completed in 1964

wood cell walls. Water vapour is taken up directly by adsorption under increased relative humidity. The consequence of wetting is that wood near the surface swells. However, the interior part of the piece responds slowly, if at all, to the moisture changes. As the surface swells and shrinks, stresses are set up in the wood due to moisture gradients between the surface and the interior. The alternating tensile and compressive stresses may cause checks and splits parallel to the grain.

The photochemical degradation of wood due to sunlight occurs fairly rapidly on the exposed wood surface and wood undergoes initial colour changes: a yellowing or browning that may proceed to eventual greying in climates with little precipitation. The changes affect only those parts of the wood close to the exposed surface and occur to a depth of 0.05–2.5 mm. These colour changes are the result of sunlight, particularly UV light, which initiates photo-degradation. Photo-degradation by UV light induces changes in the chemical composition of wood, leading principally to the degradation of lignin. Most of the dissolved lignin degradation products are washed out by rain, allowing light to penetrate deeper into the piece. Fibres high in cellulose content and whitish to grey in colour remain on the wood surface and are resistant to UV degradation.

is estimated that the surfaces of exposed softwoods erode by 3 mm per century on average (Larsen, 1994: 56).

Frequent exposure of the wood surface to rapid changes in moisture, that is, repeated wetting and drying, is one of the principal causes of weathering. Dew, rain or snow falling upon unprotected wood is quickly absorbed by capillary action on the surface layer of wood, followed by adsorption within

8.8 The patina of wood

Ideally, replacement timber should, over time, become harmonious in colour, tone, texture, form and scale with its surroundings (Feilden, 1982: 6). It can be difficult to achieve this when the patina of the existing timber is due to the effect of weathering. According to Article 12 of the Venice Charter, replacement or missing parts should integrate harmoniously with the whole, but at the same

Figure 8.10 A medieval timber structure in Telemark, Norway. The medieval logs which have not been exposed to the weather, are grey in colour and look like new timber. The external boarding, which is secondary, is dark brown in colour and has eroded due to weathering

time be distinguishable. The Wood Committee has found that, because of the characteristics of wood and its ageing process, we must take a different view when it comes to the preservation of timber structures. According to Article 10 of the Wood Committee's Principles:

It should be accepted that new members or parts of members will be distinguishable from the existing ones. To copy the natural decay or deformation of the replaced members or parts is not desirable. Appropriate traditional or well-tested modern methods may be used to match the colouring of the old and the new with

due regard that this will not harm or degrade the surface of the wooden member.

'Artificial patina' is in reality a concept without meaning for wood preservation. It is usually possible to match the colouring; to copy the natural decay and deformation of the timber is neither desirable nor attainable. However, colouring of unadorned wood using chemical or physical processes has been widely used all over the world (Kaila, 1987b: 33). Here one must consider local traditions. In England, for instance, it is advocated that repairs should be executed honestly, usually without any attempts at disguise or artificial ageing, but, on the other

Figure 8.11 Detail of the *Shakadô* hall in the Kiyomizu-dera Buddhist temple, Kyoto, Japan, built in the eighteenth century. During the dismantling–repair process, completed in 1975, the lower part of this corner pillar was repaired by jointing in new, well-seasoned timber. The new timber contrasts dramatically with the original timber, whose appearance is due to decay, insect attack and the effects of weathering

hand, repairs should not be unnecessarily obtrusive or unsympathetic in appearance (Brereton, 1995: 5). According to the experience of Japanese preservation specialists, if the new members are left untreated, the adjustment of old and new members will take place naturally over a period of twenty to thirty years (Larsen, 1994: 56). Nevertheless, the replacement of a large number of visible

members during repair would leave the building with an unsightly appearance for a long period. Japanese preservation experts have observed that the problem of matching the aesthetic appearance of new members to old ones is reduced if new members are made of similar species of wood as the existing members and, further, if they are dressed with the same tools as were used originally.

In Japan, architects and carpenters also resort to different techniques to colour new members. There is a long tradition of this even in new timber structures; as early as the seventeenth century, interior members of tea-rooms were treated in order to give them an old, rustic appearance. In Japanese preservation work today, two principal methods are used for colouring new members of unadorned wood: (1) by applying a particular coating to the surface of the member; or (2) by burning the surface of the new member with a torch followed by brushing with a steel brush.

Burning and brushing normally give good results. However, some architects are reluctant to use this method, as they believe that it shortens the durability of wood by as much as fifty years. Most architects and craftsmen in Japan favour old recipes that generally include Indian ink mixed with clay or sand, and sometimes a mineral pigment such as umber is also included. Some architects dissolve all the ingredients in animal glue or persimmon juice before applying it to the wood. The general idea is that the colouring should be relatively weak and disappear in ten to fifteen years' time, gradually allowing the new member to age naturally; that is, to acquire the desired patina.

8.9 Re-using old wood in repair work

The use of old timber from other timber structures in repair work was quite common

Figure 8.12   The Mayflower Barn, Jordans, Buckinghamshire, UK. Tradition has it that this was constructed using old timbers from the Mayflower

in days gone by. In repair work, however, the situation is different due to uncertainty about the physical and mechanical behaviour of old timbers. Most experts warn against using timber from another structure in the repair of timber-framed buildings (Charles, 1984: 58; Boutwood, 1991: 5; Brereton, 1995: 27). This is not because of any possible reduction of the strength of the timber, but due to the moral and practical difficulties in re-using old timbers from other structures in repair or replacement work. The use of second-hand timber cannibalised from old structures should be avoided because it will be archaeologically misleading. From a practical perspective, old oak is rock-hard and may well destroy tools. Furthermore, finding an exact matching piece to fit into a timber

frame is a problem in repair work. Second-hand timber brought in from other buildings may already be distorted, and such distortions can never be compatible in a different frame. According to Charles, since every structural member has individual characteristics, the chances of finding an old matching piece are slim.

We subscribe to the general scepticism towards the reuse of second-hand timber in repair work of timber frames. On the other hand, we also acknowledge that the situation may be different for other types of structures, such as log buildings, and in cultures where the reuse of old timber in repair work has a long tradition. We also see the value of the recycling of old timber carried out by professional companies, although this can have both positive and negative aspects. It is negative if an old structure is destroyed in order to obtain high-quality second-hand timber for the market for commercial reasons, because such timber may attract high prices. It is positive if companies can rescue good wood from structures that would have been destroyed anyway, and then put this timber on the market. However, in general, it should not be used for repair purposes.

9

Something nasty in the woodshed: alternatives to toxic chemicals

The use of chemical preservatives – fungicides and insecticides – in the preservation of historic timber structures should be kept to a minimum. According to Article 14 of the Wood Committee's Principles:

> *The use of chemical preservatives should be carefully controlled and monitored, and should be used only where there is an assured benefit, where public and environmental safety will not be affected and where the likelihood of success over the long term is significant.*

In other words, an approach that represents minimum intervention is always preferable. This is a way to integrate architectural preservation theory and the use of pesticides in the preservation of timber structures. We feel there are well-justified reasons to be sceptical about modern chemicals. Almost without exception, fungicides and insecticides have undesirable side effects. A prime example of this is DDT.

We suggest that, whenever possible, one should aim for an approach to pest management that includes the environment, so that conditions will prevail which are hostile for the survival of wood-decaying organisms. Some of the considerations appropriate for the control of fungi are discussed below.

9.1 Conditions for the growth of fungi and the biology of environmental control

Germination of the millions of fungal spores in the air both inside and outside buildings requires specific environmental conditions: the presence of moisture, suitable temperatures, light and air. The cardinal rule for the proper use of wood is: keep wood dry! If no water is present in the wood cell lumens of the sapwood in the timber, there will be no medium for diffusion of the wood-decomposing enzymes of fungi. Thus, as long as wood is kept below its fibre saturation point, it will not decay due to fungal attack. However, if an attack has already started, the fungi can continue to grow at humidity levels lower than the fibre saturation point, probably down to about 20 per cent of dry weight. If wood has dried out after a fungal attack, the hyphae can lie dormant for several years and start to grow again when suitable environmental conditions return.

There are, however, exceptions to the rule that wood kept below fibre saturation point is safe from fungal attack. Some fungi, such as *Serpula lacrymans*, have the unusual ability to conduct water from moist soil or other sources of moisture into dry wood. These are, consequently, called 'dry rot fungi' to distinguish

Figure 9.1 Brown rot showing typical cubical deterioration of wood

them from all the other wood-rotting fungi – 'the wet rot fungi'.

However, the role of moisture in controlling all fungal attack of wood is complicated because different stages of fungal development have different minimum requirements for moisture. Generally, more moisture is required for germination of spores than to sustain the growth of hyphae in wood, and hyphae already established in the wood can survive at moisture contents even lower than those required for actual growth. Spore germination needs free water in the wood cell lumens. Even though the wood is kept below the fibre saturation point, localised free water can occur, for example as a result of condensation, which may allow fungal infection (Bravery, 1991: 119–120).

Although temperature, air and light are also necessary for the survival and growth of fungi, the two crucial factors in sustaining outbreaks of fungal attack are water and a source of food, which is wood. Without these, even dry rot (*Serpula lacrymans*) will be severely disabled, despite its unique biological systems for adapting to the built environment. Consequently, the primary control measure in dealing with a fungal outbreak must be the restoration of dry or drying conditions. Although this may seem quite straightforward, it is more common to see people react in panic to a fungal outbreak, and in particular one of dry rot. On the advice of professional pest control companies, toxic chemicals are liberally sprayed all over the affected building, and all affected woodwork may be removed, and often woodwork that has not been affected. The real problem, however, is to locate and rectify all sources of damp and then promote the drying of the structure. The two main elements of the primary control measures are therefore (1) to locate and eliminate all sources of moisture, and (2) to promote rapid drying (Bravery, 1991: 122–123).

Secondary control measures after a dry rot attack should include (1) determining the full extent of the outbreak and the removal of rotten wood, and (2) removing all wood showing obvious evidence of fungal mycelium or softening. To avoid inclusion of active but invisible fungus in retained timbers, a safety margin can be provided by cutting back 300–450 mm into sound wood beyond the last obvious signs of attack. There is no standard specification for a mandatory cut-off depth for infected timbers. Decisions should reflect the needs in each particular case (Bravery, 1991: 124; George, 1992: 58).

(a)   (b)

Figure 9.2 (a) Urnes stave church, Sognefjord, Norway, built 1150. The northern wall with carved elements from an earlier church on the same site. One of the reasons why the wall and these ancient carvings are so well preserved is that the wall has continuously been protected using traditionally distilled pine tar. (b) Urnes stave church. Detail of an eleventh century carving

In addition, new timber must be treated, if it contains sapwood, or naturally durable timber may be selected instead. Treatment of retained timbers is not an absolute requirement, even after a dry rot attack (Bravery, 1991: 128).

9.2 Traditional wood preservation

The Greeks and Romans used oil, tars and resins, extracted from resistant timbers, to preserve structures such as bridges. The Greeks and Romans also used to protect wood that would come into contact with the ground by gently burning it in order to obtain a charred layer, which provided excellent protection for the wood. For wood preservation purposes they used various animal, vegetable and mineral oils. For example, Roman statues were treated with olive and cedar oil. Such oils are also documented as having been used by early Egyptian, Chinese and Burmese civilisations. Noah was instructed by God (Genesis 6:14) to build the Ark of gopher wood and 'pitch it within and without with pitch'.

In Norway, the use of traditionally distilled pine tar goes back to the Viking period (ninth to tenth centuries) when the Vikings used it to protect their ships. Pine tar was, and still is, made by burning pine stumps and root stocks and extracting the distillation product. From the Middle Ages up until the beginning of the twentieth century the use of pine tar was restricted to the protection of churches, since it was both time-consuming and expensive to produce. This goes a long way towards explaining why outdoor woodwork on the stave churches from the twelfth century which has been protected with pine tar is preserved in an excellent condition. Norwegian church accounts reveal that the local farmers and villagers were obliged to apply fresh tar to the external walls of the stave churches at ten-yearly intervals.

The documented use of oil paints with pigments in China goes back to 1600 BC. In Chinese literary records from the ninth to the third centuries BC, there are numerous references to the use of paint containing natural minerals, such as vermilion, cinnabar and mercury sulphate, all of which are excellent pesticides. A survey of extant Chinese timber structures from the seventh to the thirteenth century AD showed that timber columns, beams and brackets were usually covered with inorganic pigments such as burnt ochre, mineral yellow, white chalk and red ochre, and, in some cases, cinnabar, red lead, azurite or malachite were mixed with glue or gum. In medical books written before the seventh century, these pigments were all marked as poisonous and hence insect-repelling (Zhong and Chen, 1986: 304).

Of special interest is the widespread use of tung oil in China. The oil is extracted from the kernels of the tung tree (*Aleurites fordii*), a small tree native to China but cultivated in other countries with subtropical climates. The kernels yield a valuable drying oil, mainly used in paint and varnish. A record from the third century AD describes a method for the impregnation of pine by using tung oil: after felling, a large hole was made at the bottom end of the trunk and raw tung oil was poured in. The oil permeated the wood and made it strong and resistant to attack from borers. The efficacy of the method has since been proved by modern science (Zhong and Chen, 1986: 304).

Two thousand years ago, the Chinese also immersed their wood in sea water or in salt-water lakes prior to using it as a building material. During the repair work at the Hanseatic Wharf in Bergen, Norway – a World Heritage Site – the wood conservation specialist involved in the project carried out experiments by sinking new replacement timber 20 m deep in the sea to subject it to a pressure-impregnation process using sea water. This is to imitate the original timber, which has been well preserved over centuries – a fact that is partially explained by the quality of the wood and also because the original construction timber was floated by sea from where it was felled to Bergen. Furthermore, in Norway, ship masts were immersed in peat bogs before they were erected. This is extremely interesting as a possible method of preservation, as peat bogs are known for preserving organic material, including wood and human remains, for thousands of years.

Interesting alternatives to the highly toxic industrial chemical wood preservatives may be found in traditional remedies, some of which are mentioned above. Another example can be found in Kudus, a city located in central Java, Indonesia, where preserved timber structures with remarkable carved decorations are to be found. The houses are well-preserved as the result of a religious ritual performed once a year, at the end of Ramadan. At this time, the local population believes that everything must be cleansed, including the exterior of the houses. The houses are built of teak (*Tectona grandis*), a timber of excellent natural durability. The climate, however, is hot and humid, and the wood would eventually decay as a result of fungal attack or deteriorate due to termite attack if it were not for the annual cleansing ritual. In reality, this is a wood preservation rite. The local people use either a solution of tobacco (*Nicotiana tabacum*) or cloves (*Eugenia aromatica*) in water. The solution is applied to the whole of the house exterior with a brush made from black sugar palm fibre, and the brushing continues for some time. The result is that the colour of the teak timbers changes from greyish to brown, similar to the original colour. The other effect, confirmed by laboratory tests, is that the treatment is both fungicidal and insecticidal, as it prevents termite attacks. However, it has been noted that the tradition may disappear as the professionals who were involved in this practice are getting older and the younger generation is reluctant to do this kind of hard work (Samidi *et al.,* 1993).

9.3 Industrial wood preservation

The Industrial Revolution in England saw the 'final solution' of the wood preservation problem. The development of the steam engine provided engineers with the technology to build tanks that could withstand high pressure. At the same time the coal industry was under development and factories made a number of products from coal, such as creosote. The year 1838 marks the start of industrial wood preservation, when John Bethell invented and patented a process of impregnating wood with protective fluids under high pressure. He used creosote as a pesticide. Creosote, therefore, is the oldest industrial preservative still in use for impregnation of, for example, utility poles.

At the beginning of the twentieth century, research began on wood preservatives based on water-soluble salts. The problem with using water-soluble salts is that the salts eventually dissolve and are washed out of the wood during use. The problem was solved by Indian chemists in the 1930s who developed a salt impregnation method based on copper, chromium and arsenic salts (CCA) which were dissolved in water and forced into the wood under high pressure (Connell, 1991: 19). The three salts are introduced into the wood as a water-soluble mixture which then reacts in such a way as to render them water-insoluble. This enables the treated timber to be used in damp or wet conditions without subsequent loss of protection by leaching. However, it is in fact sapwood which is impregnated through the CCA pressure impregnation method. Heartwood cannot be impregnated. Therefore it is essential in the repair of historic buildings to use heartwood, in order to avoid using sapwood which must be impregnated with CCA or other dangerous substances.

Neither oil-based nor water-based industrial wood preservatives can yet replace the CCA method, although a number of chemicals have been tried. Attempts to replace the arsenic compounds in CCA solutions with fluorides, borates or fluoroborates have only been partially effective. The boron compounds and the fluorides remain water-soluble throughout their service lives and are therefore prone to leaching if placed in environments where water can permeate the wood. Increasingly, the use of chromium is also coming under scrutiny. It seems that only copper is likely to remain as the principal fungicidal component in most future industrial water-based preservation systems (Connell, 1991: 28–30).

Boron constitutes about 0.001 per cent of the weight of the Earth's crust. In the form of boric acids (H_3BO_3) or borates, traces of boron are necessary for growth of land plants. Borates have a wide spectrum of fungicidal and insecticidal efficacy, coupled with relatively low mammalian toxicity. Borate-treated wood is unchanged in colour, non-corrosive to fasteners, has increased fire resistance and can be easily glued and finished. However, borates have one major disadvantage in that they do not chemically adhere to the wood structure and so are prone to leaching under exposed conditions. As soon as borate-treated wood comes into contact with water, the borates are dissolved, and they no longer have a toxic effect on fungi and insects. When borates are dissolved there are further problems with their efflorescent salts, which have been shown to be capable of destroying adjacent masonry materials (Weaver, 1993: 55).

Borates act as a slow-acting poison to insects and a contact poison which causes fungi to decay. Borates can be used to treat new wood, and also existing timber in structures. Pesticides containing borates may be applied as sprays or by pressure injecting solutions or foams. A convenient method in both new and old timber is the use of borate impel rods. Holes are drilled in the wood and the rods are inserted according to the manufacturer's calculations, taking into account the size of the wood and the amount of boric acid needed to protect the wood. The rods contain boric acid which is absorbed by the wood when the moisture content of the wood exceeds 25 per cent. When wood is dry, the boric acid is inactive.

9.4 The Integrated Pest Management approach

Through the 1980s and 1990s, there has been a marked move away from the practice of pouring chemicals into trouble-spots in the belief that this would solve the problem, as in the treatment of dry rot (*Serpula lacrymans*) mentioned above. Today, the perspective has changed. Attacks by dry rot, considered by many as the most dangerous and destructive of the wood-decaying fungi, and termites, likewise considered by many to be the gravest insect-threat to historic buildings globally, may today be dealt with by a comprehensive strategy of Integrated Pest Management (IPM).

The history of dry rot is in itself revealing for the necessity to see life processes in a global perspective. In the wild, *Serpula lacrymans* grows on tree stumps between 3000 and 5000 m up in the Himalayan forests. In Europe and North America the fungus is purely domestic, thriving on damp conditions inside houses. The fungus reached the UK during the second half of the eighteenth century, probably on batches of softwoods imported to supplement native hardwoods in order to meet the increasing demand for new housing and ships. Contemporary writers were baffled by this new form of rot, which seemed to attack from the inside out and left wood dry and brittle. It was soon christened 'dry rot' (George, 1992: 49; Carlstrand, 1998).

IPM may be defined as a sustainable approach to pest management by combining biological, cultural, physical and chemical tools in a way that minimises economic, health and environmental risks. The concept has been developed within agricultural pest control. From the first philosophical description of integrated control in the late 1950s, IPM has expanded, particularly in the USA, to encompass major efforts in research and implementation. Gradually, in the USA as well as elsewhere, the idea of IPM has also spread to the preservation of historic buildings. As an example of the application of IPM, let us see how the strategy may be applied to termite control in the four forms of cultural, physical, biological and chemical control.

All types of termites need moisture. Consequently, the major element in cultural control is to keep structures dry and ventilated. To prevent attack from subterranean termites, sub-floor areas should be ventilated. Paving around the structure should be angled to drain surface water away from the structure. Structural wood should be kept from contact with the ground. Any timber or cellulose material stored beneath a suspended floor should be removed. To prevent attacks from dry-wood termites, cracks should be sealed, although this may be impracticable in historic structures where old timber normally has cracks. We cannot recommend any types of synthetic resins for filling cracks. If the cracks are filled, the wood will still continue to swell and shrink, and the non-flexible epoxies will not follow these movements, which may lead to further cracking elsewhere in the timber. Moreover, we have no control over what may happen in the interface between the resin and the wood; for instance, water may accumulate. If the historic timber originally had some surface treatment or coating, such as paint or varnish, this practice should be continued.

To prevent attack from subterranean termites, the strategy of physical control is basically to separate the termites from their source of food. Several physical ground barriers are marketed. Termites may also be controlled by taking their environment beyond the limits their body can withstand. Sustained heat – more than 45 degrees centigrade for more than an hour – and sustained cold have both been used. A 'gun' which delivers high voltages (90 000 volts) and low current has successfully been developed by a US company for the eradication of dry-wood termites. Using timber that is naturally durable and resistant to fungal decay and insect attacks appears to be an age-old tradi-

tion all over the world. Unfortunately, we may not always be able to continue these practices, as the forest resources that provided these timbers may have been depleted. As mentioned previously, this is the major reason why the Wood Committee has proposed the establishment of Historic Forest Reserves.

There is much interesting research going on in the field of biological control, although as yet without substantial practical success. In some traditional societies, people have used birds and ants, natural enemies of the termites, to keep them in check. The wood preservation industry is now testing the efficacy for wood preservation of biocides developed in other sectors, such as in agriculture. However, these new, presumably environmentally friendly agrochemicals tend to be organism-specific and are designed to biodeteriorate rapidly in ground contact. These properties are not necessarily compatible with efficient wood preservation.

Until recently, chemical control was the only solution offered by pest controllers to the termite problem. However, during the past few years several of the chemicals used have been banned in most countries. Newly introduced chemicals are also coming under increasing scrutiny. Chemical control for subterranean termites has included soil treatment to provide a chemical barrier of toxic residues. For dry-wood termites the use of tenting, and flooding the structure with a toxic fumigant, some of which may be damaging to the ozone layer, are methods that have been tried. Another way to use chemicals is to apply them directly to the termites, such as in the 'bait box technique'. Bait boxes can be used inside, under or around buildings. Termite baiting should only be used as part of an Integrated Pest Management strategy, where destruction of the termite colony will be followed by hazard reduction and regular inspection.

9.5 Biochemical and biological approaches to wood preservation

Using biochemical and biological means to control pests in timber structures is a recent development, but one which clearly offers the most environmentally friendly approach to wood preservation. However, knowledge and experience of these methods is, at present, limited. The biochemical approach to protection against fungal attacks operates on the principle of making wood indigestible to the fungi instead of poisoning the wood. This approach starts with the study of the metabolism of the fungi, and research is being done into fungi's use of enzymes and other types of catalysts to break down the wood polymers (Kersten *et al.*, 1995; Whittaker *et al.*, 1996).

An example of a biological approach to wood preservation is a study made at St Nicholas church and bell-tower in the Kovda village in Murmansk in northern Russia. The church and the bell-tower are log structures; the church was probably built in the latter half of the seventeenth century. Three species of wood-destroying fungi, including the dry rot fungus (*Serpula lacrymans*), were found to be active during an inspection by two biologists during 1991–2. The biologists also found that a fourth fungus, *Trichoderma viride*, had infected the logs of the two buildings. However, this fungus only causes surface damage to wood and has a remarkable additional characteristic: it can stop the growth of dangerous wood-decaying fungi. It excretes a biologically active substance that is poisonous to many other fungi species, including *Serpula lacrymans*. The biologists concluded that the effect of *Trichoderma viride*, together with good ventilation, has promoted the natural conservation of the monument. The biologists tried to prevent a proposal to treat the church and bell-tower with chemical preservatives, which would have destroyed this delicate biological balance, but unfortunately they did not succeed (Kudrjavtseva *et al.*, 1995).

9.6 Protective paints and coatings

It is also worth considering the various paint systems that were designed to protect wood. A traditional paint based on, for example, linseed oil, saturates the outer layer of wood cells so that water cannot penetrate easily into the wood, but allows water that has accumulated inside to evaporate. Article 7 of the Wood Committee's Principles recommends that when renewing surface finishes such as paints, the original materials, techniques and textures should be duplicated as far as possible.

Modern paint systems may have a detrimental effect on wood. In the 1980s a century-old log building, part of a well-known hotel in Norway, was undergoing repair and restoration. The logs were in good condition before the work started. The owner was advised to paint the exposed timber walls with an acrylic paint; the paint manufacturer even advised using an extra thick layer to ensure maximum protection. The protection from external penetration of water may have been excellent, but water can also come from the inside, which was what happened in this case. Because of the impenetrable plastic paint layer, the humidity could not escape and was trapped inside the logs. The result was that, within a year, the damage due to decay was so severe that a major restoration project had to be implemented, wherein the damaged logs were replaced with new timber by an expert restoration carpenter. If the owner had followed the advice of the Wood Committee's Principles concerning surface treatments, large amounts of the original material and a large amount of money would have been saved.

10

The past has power: sustainable development – learning from historic timber structures

A living society is in continuous change. It is important for the quality of life that this change process is controlled and that existing values are brought to the fore. If people are going to make the important choices necessary for sustainable development, they have to see themselves as part of a continuum with obligations for future generations. Our cultural heritage is an important element in the creation of this understanding. Cultural heritage can be regarded as knowledge in a material form about sustainable production and consumption, and this knowledge forms an important basis for the development of society, and is a prerequisite for accountable resource management.

The World Commission on Environment and Development (WCED)'s report (1987) defines sustainable development as 'development which meets the needs of the present without compromising the ability of future generations to meet their own needs'. The first article in WCED's proposed Legal Principles for Environmental Protection and Sustainable Development states that 'All human beings have the fundamental right to an environment adequate for their health and well-being'. Although this shows that the WCED report focuses on quality issues as well as natural environment issues, the definition of sustainable development is today

almost solely used in a natural environment context.

The UK's Environment White Paper (1990) amplifies the WCED definition:

Sustainable development means living on the Earth's income rather than eroding its capital. It means keeping the consumption of renewable natural resources within the limits of their replenishment. It means handing down to successive generations not only man-made wealth, but also natural wealth, such as clean and adequate water supplies, good arable land, a wealth of wildlife, and ample forests.

Sustainability can only be obtained if the solutions chosen are simultaneously ecologically viable, economically feasible and socially desirable. If the balance among these criteria is not reasonable, it is likely that the desired outcome will not be sustainable because of failure in one or more of the three areas.

10.1 Learning from the past

If our intention is to create a sustainable society, we can learn three things from old

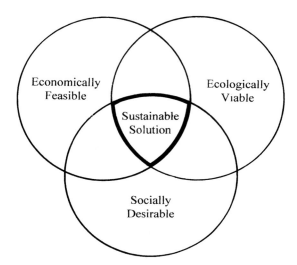

Figure 10.1 Sustaining desired ecosystem conditions requires that management goals and actions fall within the intersection of three spheres: that they be simultaneously ecologically viable (environmentally sound), economically feasible (affordable) and socially desirable (politically acceptable). (After Salwasser *et al.*, 1990)

timber structures that can be applied with benefit to contemporary construction work. Firstly, the traditional knowledge and selection of materials were based on a deep understanding of nature and of the uses and limitations of natural materials, such as wood. Previous generations did not have access to the chemical wood preservatives of today, but relied on the natural durability of wood, that is, they used the heartwood of durable species. Acquiring this knowledge and understanding of wood would benefit both the present generation and our successors in our aim to create long-lasting timber structures.

Market forces and public opinion contribute to sustainable development. Naturally durable wood may be compared to organically produced food, which is becoming increasingly widespread and popular. An increasing number of people are willing to pay more for high-quality products. The same

may also apply to traditional building materials that are selected and used in order to reduce the use of toxic chemicals. Traditional materials need not necessarily be more expensive. Smaller suppliers with low-scale investments may exploit the emerging interest in traditional materials to find a market niche not covered by the larger suppliers, which depend on large quantities to maintain a good business turnover.

Secondly, we believe that the use of the old techniques of craftsmanship based on manual labour may be attractive in niche markets where people want high-quality products. In fact, only by increasing the number of craftsmen able to produce traditional timber structures at relatively competitive prices will we have craftsmen who can repair historic timber structures. In Japan, there is a market for new buildings in old styles, and there is even a special architectural journal for this purpose called *Residential Architecture* (Jutaku kenchiku). In Norway, an increasing number of specialised building firms are trying to meet a similar growing demand for traditionally built houses.

An interesting example of the competitiveness of traditional timber structures is the rebuilding of the wooden cupola and roofs over St Catherine's church in Stockholm after a fire in 1990. The church had been built in 1723. Architect Professor Ove Hidemark and civil engineer Krister Berggren were responsible for the design for the rebuilding of the church. Berggren considered the question of durability before suggesting methods for the reconstruction of the church (Berggren, 1994). He said that St Catherine's church had existed for 300 years; other Swedish churches were 900 years old. How long should a church be expected to last – perhaps 500 years? In contemporary buildings, the average life expectancy of structures and parts is estimated at thirty to fifty years.

SKALA
10 0 1 2 3 4 5 6 7 8 9 10   15   20M

OVE HIDEM/

Figure 10.2 St Catherine's church, Stockholm, Sweden. Section. (Drawing from Ove Hidemark Arkitektkontor AB)

The building committee agreed that they should put a 500-year perspective on the rebuilding. Thus, they ruled out concrete which, in certain environments, may deteriorate completely within twenty years. No glues in use today have existed for more than fifty years. Today's gluelam structures may have sufficient durability for buildings with a 'normal' life expectancy, but could hardly be expected to last for 500 years. A steel structure was considered, but was ruled out for practical and financial reasons.

One of Sweden's larger contractors, with only limited experience in working with historic buildings and historical technology, was hired for the project. An expert on traditional carpentry showed the contractor's carpenters how to make the roof trusses in the traditional way and how to cut joints using an axe. However, some compromises to modern technology had to be made, as the carpenters lacked the necessary experience to handle the axes effectively. Thus, in order to achieve the aim of the project – which was to employ traditional materials and traditional structural techniques for the sake of the long-term preservation of the building – at an acceptable cost, some modern construction tools and equipment had to be employed. In the main, however, this project became a testing ground for the technology of the seventeenth and eighteenth centuries. The project proved that this technology was not only exciting and inspiring, but also, economically speaking, a competitor or rival to the so-called better solutions of contemporary building technology (Hidemark, 1996).

Thirdly, from the perspective of sustainable development, it is interesting to observe that old buildings may be more environmentally friendly than modern ones. Faced with growing pollution and global environmental problems, the Norwegian building industry aims to create sustainable solutions for the future. In this respect, a great deal of atten-tion has so far been focused on energy saving. However, this in itself is not sufficient, and a comprehensive life-cycle analysis will give a better understanding of the total environmental consequences of a building project. Life-cycle analysis quantifies energy and material usage, and air and liquid emissions as well as the solid waste generated at each stage of a product's life cycle. These stages include:

1. resource extraction;
2. manufacture;
3. construction;
4. service;
5. post-use disposal.

Thus, life-cycle analysis provides an analysis and assessment of the environmental effects of a building's materials, components and assemblies throughout the entire life of the building. Life-cycle analysis examines the full range of impacts over all the phases of a product's life, instead of focusing on any specific stage (Canadian Wood Council, 1997).

10.2 Environmental impact in a life-cycle perspective: a case study

In a recent study by the Norwegian Building Research Institute, in co-operation with the Norwegian Directorate for Cultural Heritage, a traditional log building was compared with a modern, fully insulated timber-frame building of the same size (Fossdal and Edvardsen, 1995). Today, 98 per cent of Norwegian low-rise housing is of timber-frame construction. Log houses, on the other hand, dominated Norwegian building traditions from the Viking period and well into the twentieth century, in towns as well as in the countryside. As a result, most of Norway's historic buildings are log buildings.

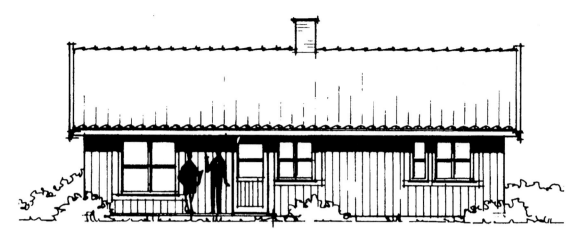

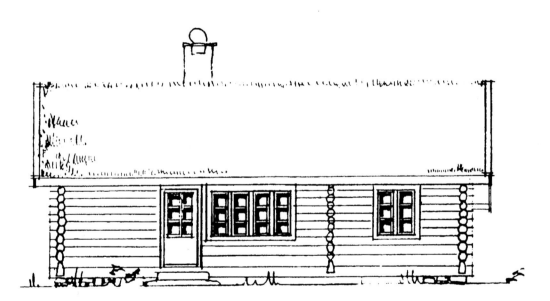

Figure 10.3 Contemporary Norwegian timber-frame house (*upper*) and log house. (After Fossdal and Edvardsen, 1995)

Of the two houses compared in the Norwegian study, the timber-frame house had walls with 150 mm of mineral wool insulation, an external wind barrier of 12 mm bitumen-impregnated porous fibreboard and a vapour barrier on the inside of 0.15 mm polythene film. The internal lining was 13 mm plasterboard. The floors and roof were insulated with 200 mm mineral wool. The external walls of the log-house were a traditional log-construction, using logs about 16 cm diameter at their thickest. No external or internal insulation, boarding or film were added. What advantages did the one have

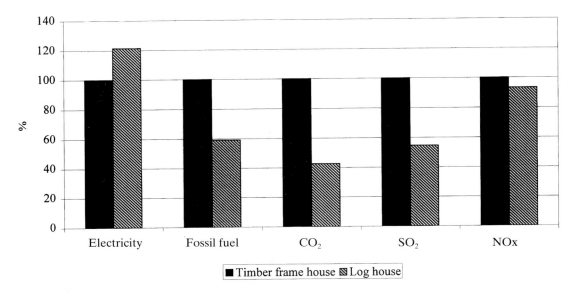

Figure 10.4   Normalised consumption and emissions for the timber-frame house and the log house. (After Fossdal and Edvardsen, 1995)

over the other, both buildings being of the same size? It was assumed that both houses would be heated using electricity. The calculations were carried out based on the climatic conditions in Oslo, which has relatively cold winters.

The study found that the traditional log house had far less impact on the environment in almost every aspect than the modern, fully insulated timber-frame house. For example, the global warming potential of the timber-frame house, expressed in CO_2 equivalents, was more than double that of the log house. The building materials used in the log house are mainly naturally sustainable materials and are to a certain extent used in their natural form and therefore create a minimum of waste. The negative side of the log house was that the total energy consumption was 20 per cent higher compared to the fully insulated modern house.

This study showed that preserving existing log buildings and building new houses using this traditional technique could contribute towards a sustainable future. Indeed, many people, both in the countryside and in the suburbs of the towns, are building traditional log houses. The carpentry techniques which are necessary to build log buildings are today practised by carpenters all over Norway. Moreover, the sustainable knowledge embedded in the historic timber structures could be used in the development of contemporary building techniques.

Good or sustainable administration of the current building stock is of decisive significance for the use of resources and the reduction of waste and discharge. Administration of the building stock requires knowledge which in some cases has been lost. A number of environmentally friendly materials that were used in days gone by are no longer manufactured. Professional interest within the building sector has concentrated on new construction for many years. Faith in new materials has been strong and the need to learn from previous experience has been small. One indicator of this is that in Norway

(a)

Figure 10.5 (a) River and Rowing Museum, Henley, England. Architect David Chipperfield (1996). The green-oak cladding was carefully selected for economy and durability. (b) Detail

in around 1900 there were less than fifty different materials in use in the construction industry, all tried and tested with proven strengths and weaknesses. A hundred years later, there are at least 40 000 materials on the market. For the vast majority, no information is available about their characteristics or long-term functionality.

In the future, new requirements will be laid down regarding buildings and building materials. Currently, such requirements are largely concerned with their qualities in use,

(b)

while in the future stipulations will be made regarding qualities in a life-cycle perspective. This means that a building's energy consumption will no longer be calculated for the period that the building is actually in use, but will be calculated for the whole life cycle of the building, that is to say, from the time the building is designed until it is torn down. This means that the energy costs involved in the production and destruction of the materials will have to be included in the energy calculations. For example, the manufacture of cement and mineral wool requires a great deal of energy, and therefore the energy consumption in the production phase must be weighed up against the energy gain obtained by insulating using mineral wool.

The costs involved in destruction will also be taken into account. Constructions that can easily be dismantled will be preferable to complicated constructions with a lot of waste products. Traditional building technology comprises, for the most part, simple constructions, using few materials, which in turn increases the opportunities for re-use and reduces the amount of waste products.

Furthermore, when the focus shifts from quick profits to the long-term durability of buildings and houses, traditional knowledge may also offer viable alternatives. Our built heritage shows that by using traditional construction techniques and well-known materials, it is possible to construct and maintain buildings in a way that will make them last for hundreds of years. Traditional materials and construction techniques have more advantages in the context of sustainable development. Traditional structures are often simple and easy to repair, and allow easy replacement of any damaged or worn-out materials. It is also easy to separate the building materials during demolition of traditional structures, which increases the potential to recycle the material. Finally, most traditional building materials can be produced locally, reducing transportation costs, and thereby also reducing the total impact on the environment (Myhre, 1996).

We are now at a time in history when historic timber structures have become important not only for their own sake but also as patterns for contemporary construction. At the start of the twenty-first century, the movement towards 'alternative buildings' or 'green buildings' is gaining momentum. There is an increasing demand for traditional, natural, sustainable building products and services. The ideal is to live in harmony, instead of in conflict with nature. There is an increasing interest in cultures attuned to their natural surroundings and in environmentally responsible design and construction. These are precisely the fields where our heritage of historic timber structures can act as a superb reservoir of knowledge, if only we can learn to interpret its message correctly.

Appendix

Principles for the Preservation of Historic Timber Structures

Adopted by ICOMOS International Wood Committee in Datong, China, June 1998
Accepted by ICOMOS General Assembly in Guadalajara, Mexico, October 1999

The aim of this document is to define basic and universally applicable principles and practices for the protection and preservation of historic timber structures with due respect to their cultural significance. Historic timber structures refer here to all types of buildings or constructions wholly or partially in timber that have cultural significance or that are parts of an historic area.

For the purpose of the preservation of such structures, the Principles:

- *recognise* the importance of timber structures from all periods as part of the cultural heritage of the world;
- *take into account* the great diversity of historic timber structures;
- *take into account* the various species and qualities of wood used to build them;
- *recognise* the vulnerability of structures wholly or partially in timber due to material decay and degradation in varying environmental and climatic conditions, caused by humidity fluctuations, light, fungal and insect attacks, wear and tear, fire and other disasters;
- *recognise* the increasing scarcity of historic timber structures due to vulnerability, misuse and the loss of skills and knowledge of traditional design and construction technology;
- *take into account* the great variety of actions and treatments required for the preservation and conservation of these heritage resources;
- *note* the Venice Charter, the Burra Charter and related UNESCO and ICOMOS doctrine, and seek to apply these general principles to the protection and preservation of historic timber structures;
- *make* the following recommendations:

Inspection, recording and documentation

1. The condition of the structure and its components should be carefully recorded before any intervention, as well as all materials used in treatments, in accordance with Article 16 of the Venice Charter and the ICOMOS Principles for the Recording of Monuments, Groups of Buildings and Sites. All pertinent

documentation, including characteristic samples of redundant materials or members removed from the structure, and information about relevant traditional skills and technologies, should be collected, catalogued, securely stored and made accessible as appropriate. The documentation should also include the specific reasons given for choice of materials and methods in the preservation work.

2. A thorough and accurate diagnosis of the condition and the causes of decay and structural failure of the timber structure should precede any intervention. The diagnosis should be based on documentary evidence, physical inspection and analysis, and, if necessary, measurements of physical conditions and non-destructive testing methods. This should not prevent necessary minor interventions and emergency measures.

Monitoring and maintenance

3. A coherent strategy of regular monitoring and maintenance is crucial for the protection of historic timber structures and their cultural significance.

Interventions

4. The primary aim of preservation and conservation is to maintain the historical authenticity and integrity of the cultural heritage. Each intervention should therefore be based on proper studies and assessments. Problems should be solved according to relevant conditions and needs with due respect for the aesthetic and historical values, and the physical integrity of the historic structure or site.

5. Any proposed intervention should for preference:

a) follow traditional means;
b) be reversible, if technically possible; or
c) at least not prejudice or impede future preservation work whenever this may become necessary;
d) not hinder the possibility of later access to evidence incorporated in the structure.

6. The minimum intervention in the fabric of an historic timber structure is an ideal. In certain circumstances, minimum intervention can mean that their preservation and conservation may require the complete or partial dismantling and subsequent re-assembly in order to allow for the repair of timber structures.

7. In the case of interventions, the historic structure should be considered as a whole; all material, including structural members, in-fill panels, weather-boarding, roofs, floors, doors and windows, etc., should be given equal attention. In principle, as much as possible of the existing material should be retained. The protection should also include surface finishes such as plaster, paint, coating, wallpaper, etc. If it is necessary to renew or replace surface finishes, the original materials, techniques and textures should be duplicated as far as possible.

8. The aim of restoration is to conserve the historic structure and its load-bearing function and to reveal its cultural values by improving the legibility of its historical integrity, its earlier state and design within the limits of existing historic material evidence, as indicated in articles 9–13 of the Venice Charter. Removed members and other components of the historic structure should be catalogued, and characteristic samples kept in permanent storage as part of the documentation.

Repair and replacement

9. In the repair of an historic structure, replacement timber can be used with due respect to relevant historical and aesthetic values, and where it is an appropriate response to the need to replace decayed or damaged members or their parts, or to the requirements of restoration.

   New members or parts of members should be made of the same species of wood with the same, or, if appropriate, with better, grading as in the members being replaced. Where possible, this should also include similar natural characteristics. The moisture content and other physical characteristics of the replacement timber should be compatible with the existing structure.

   Craftsmanship and construction technology, including the use of dressing tools or machinery, should, where possible, correspond with those used originally. Nails and other secondary materials should, where appropriate, duplicate the originals.

   If a part of a member is replaced, traditional woodwork joints should, if appropriate and compatible with structural requirements, be used to splice the new and the existing part.

10. It should be accepted that new members or parts of members will be distinguishable from the existing ones. To copy the natural decay or deformation of the replaced members or parts is not desirable. Appropriate traditional or well-tested modern methods may be used to match the colouring of the old and the new with due regard that this will not harm or degrade the surface of the wooden member.

11. New members or parts of members should be discretely marked, by carving, by marks burnt into the wood or by other methods, so that they can be identified later.

'Historic Forest Reserves'

12. The establishment and protection of forest or woodland reserves where appropriate timber can be obtained for the preservation and repair of historic timber structures should be encouraged.

    Institutions responsible for the preservation and conservation of historic structures and sites should establish or encourage the establishment of stores of timber appropriate for such work.

Contemporary materials and technologies

13. Contemporary materials, such as epoxy resins, and techniques, such as structural steel reinforcement, should be chosen and used with the greatest caution, and only in cases where the durability and structural behaviour of the materials and construction techniques have been satisfactorily proven over a sufficiently long period of time. Utilities, such as heating, and fire detection and prevention systems, should be installed with due recognition of the historic and aesthetic significance of the structure or site.

14. The use of chemical preservatives should be carefully controlled and monitored, and should be used only where there is an assured benefit, where public and environmental safety will not be affected and where the likelihood of success over the long term is significant.

Education and training

15. Regeneration of values related to the cultural significance of historic timber structures through educational programmes is an essential requisite of a

sustainable preservation and development policy. The establishment and further development of training programmes on the protection, preservation and conservation of historic timber structures are encouraged. Such training should be based on a comprehensive strategy integrated within the needs of sustainable production and consumption, and include programmes at the local, national, regional and international levels. The programmes should address all relevant professions and trades involved in such work, and, in particular, architects, conservators, engineers, craftsmen and site managers.

References

Ashurst, J. and Ashurst, N. (1988) *Practical Building Conservation. Volume 5: Wood, Glass and Resins. English Heritage Technical Handbook.* Aldershot: Gower Technical Press Ltd.

Baldassino, N., Piazza, M. and Zanon, P. (1996) In Situ Evaluation of the Mechanical Properties of Timber Structural Elements. In: *10th International Symposium on Nondestructive Testing of Wood. Lausanne, Switzerland, 26–28 August 1996. Proceedings.* Lausanne: Presses polytechniques et universitaires romandes, pp. 369–377.

Berg, A. (1989) *Norske tømmerhus frå mellomalderen. Allment oversyn.* Oslo: Landbruksforlaget.

Berggren, K. (1994) Katarina kyrka. Återuppbyggnaden efter branden. *Kulturmiljövård*, 2–3, 72–78.

Blanchette, R. A., Nilsson, T., Daniel, G. and Abad, A. (1990) Biological Degradation of Wood. In: *Archaeological Wood. Properties, Chemistry and Preservation* (R. M. Rowell and R. J. Barbour, eds). Washington, DC: American Chemical Society, pp. 141–174.

Bonamini, G. (1995) Restoring timber structures – inspection and evaluation. In: *Timber Engineering. STEP 2* (H. J. Blass *et al.*, eds). Centrum Hout, The Netherlands, pp. D3/1–9.

Borgin, K. (1971) The mechanism of the breakdown of the structure of wood due to environmental factors. *Institute of Wood Science Journal*, 4, 26–30.

Boutwood, J. (1991) *The Repair of Timber Frames and Roofs.* London: Society for the Protection of Ancient Buildings. Technical pamphlet 12.

Boutwood, J. (1992) Original Structure and the Effects of Alteration and Repair. In: *ICOMOS UK: Timber Engineering Conference, Surrey University, 8 April. Proceedings.* London: ICOMOS UK.

Bravery, A. F. (1991) The Strategy for Eradication of *Serpula lacrymans*. In: *Serpula lacrymans. Fundamental Biology and Control Strategies* (D.H. Jennings and A.F. Bravery, eds). Chichester: John Wiley & Sons, pp. 117–130.

Brereton, C. (1995) *The Repair of Historic Buildings.* London: English Heritage.

Brown, S. A. (1989) *The Genius of Japanese Carpentry.* Tokyo and New York: Kodansha International.

Canadian Wood Council (1997) Comparing the Environmental Effects of Building Systems. *Wood the Renewable Resource 4.* Ottawa: Canadian Wood Council.

Carlstrand, V. (1998) The horror from the Himalayas. *FT Property (Financial Times)*, 21–22 March, pp. 1–2.

Charles, F. W. B. with Charles, M. (1984) *Conservation of Timber Buildings.* London: Hutchinson.

Charles, F. W. B. (1992) Dismantling, Repairing and Rebuilding as a Means of Conservation. In: *ICOMOS UK: Timber Engineering Conference, Surrey University, 8 April. Proceedings.* London: ICOMOS UK.

Chilton, J. E. (1995) History of timber structures. In: *Timber Engineering. STEP 2* (H. J. Blass *et al.*, eds) E1/1–13. Centrum Hout, The Netherlands.

Choay, F. (1995) Sept propositions sur le concept d'authenticité et son usage dans les pratiques du patrimoine historique. In: *Nara Conference on Authenticity/Conference de Nara sur l'Authenticité. Proceedings/Compte-rendu* (K. E. Larsen, ed.). Trondheim/Tokyo: Tapir Publishers/ Agency for Cultural Affairs, Japan, pp. 101–120.

Connell, M. (1991) Industrial Wood Preservatives – The History, Development, Use, Advantages, and Future Trends. In: *The Chemistry of Wood Preservation* (R. Thompson, ed.). Cambridge: The Royal Society of Chemistry, pp. 16–33.

Davey, N. (1961) *A History of Building Materials.* London: Phoenix House.

Dvorak, M. (1916) *Katechismus der Denkmalpflege.* Vienna: Verlag von Julius Bard.

European Standard EN 350-2 (1994) *Durability of Wood and Wood-based Products – Natural Durability of Solid Wood, Part 2: Guide to Natural Durability and Treatability of Selected Wood Species of Importance in Europe.*

Feilden, B. M. (1982) *Conservation of Historic Buildings.* London: Butterworth Scientific.

Feilden, B. M. (1984) A Possible Ethic for the Conservation of Timber Structures. In:

Conservation of Timber Buildings (Charles, F. W. B. with Charles, M., eds). London: Hutchinson, pp. 238–241.

Feist, W. C. and Hon, D. N-S. (1984) Chemistry of Weathering and Protection. In: *The Chemistry of Solid Wood*, Advances in Chemistry Series 207 (R. Rowell, ed.). Washington, DC: American Chemical Society, pp. 401–451.

Fengel, D. (1991) Aging and fossilization of wood and its components. *Wood Science and Technology*, 5: 3, 153–177.

Fossdal, S. and Edvardsen, K. I. (1995) *Energy Consumption and Environmental Impact of Buildings*. Oslo: Norwegian Building Research Institute, Project Report 177–1995.

George, C. J. D. (1992) The Conservative Repair and Treatment of Timber in Historic Buildings. In: *B.W.P.D.A. Annual Convention 1992*, pp. 45–60.

Gerner, M. (1979) *Fachwerk. Entwicklung, Gefüge, Instandsetzung*. Stuttgart: Deutsche Verlags-Anstalt.

Gerner, M. (1994) Case Study: Restoration Work on Non-stable Timberwork. *Crafts and Heritage*, 8, 7–18.

Haslestad, A. (1991) Middelalderprogrammet. In: *Vern og virke. Årsberetning fra Riksantikaren*. Oslo: Riksantikvaren, pp. 38–39.

Haslestad, A. (1993a) Gamle håndverkstradisjoner gjenopplives. *Fortidsvern* 1, 13–18.

Haslestad, A. (1993b) Middelalderprogrammet. In: *Teknisk bygningsvern*. Oslo: Norges forskningsråd, pp. 38–39.

Hewett, C. A. (1969) *The Development of Carpentry, 1200–1700. An Essex Study*. New York: Augustus M. Kelley Publishers.

Hidemark, O. (1994) Traditionell byggnadsteknik – marginalkunnskap eller baskunnskap? *Kulturmiljövård*, 2/3, 6–9.

Hidemark, O. (1996) En studie av gammal träbyggnadsteknik i kombination med nutida formgivning. In: *Arkitektur i trä. Träpriset 1996*. Stockholm: Träinformation, pp. 141–157.

Hillis, W. E. (1987) *Heartwood and Tree Exudates*. Berlin: Springer-Verlag.

Hoadley, R. B. (1990) *Identifying Wood*. Newtown: The Taunton Press, Inc.

Holmström, I. (1993) Restaureringsideologiarna och det hantverksbaserade underhållet. *Nordisk arkitekturforskning*, 1, 7–22.

ICOMOS (1990) *Summary Report. 9th General Assembly and International Symposium*. Lausanne: ICOMOS Switzerland.

Jokilehto, J. (1986) *A History of Architectural Conservation. The Contribution of English, French, German and Italian Thought towards an International Approach to the Conservation of Cultural Property*. PhD dissertation: The University of York, The Institute of Advanced Architectural Studies.

Kaila, P. (1987a) Sunshine – the worst enemy of wooden facades. In: *ICOMOS 8th General Assembly and International Symposium. Symposium Papers, Volume 1*. Washington, DC: US ICOMOS, pp. 333–337.

Kaila, P. (1987b) Byggnadsteknik. In: *Byggnadskonservering. Handbok för restaurering av byggnader som bevaras för museiändamål* (P. Kaila, T. Vihavainen, and P. Ekbom, eds). Helsinki: Finlands museiförbund, pp. 4–114.

Kaneta, K. (1978) Structural Reinforcement of Wooden Buildings. In: *International Symposium on the Conservation and Restoration of Cultural Property – Conservation of Wood*. Tokyo: Tokyo National Research Institute of Cultural Properties, pp. 95–125.

Kersten, P. J., Witek, C., Wymelenberg, A. W. and Cullen, D. (1995) *Phanerochaete chrysosporium* Glyoxal Oxidase is Encoded by Two Allelic Variants: Structure, Genomic Organization, and Herologous Expression of glx1 and glx2. *Journal of Bacteriology*, November, pp. 6106–6110.

Kirk, T. K. and Cowling, E. B. (1984) Biological Decomposition of Solid Wood. In: *The Chemistry of Solid Wood*, Advances in Chemistry Series 207 (R. Rowell, ed.). Washington, DC: American Chemical Society, pp. 455–487.

Kohara, J. (1954) Studies on the permanence of wood – VI. *The Scientific Reports of the Saikyo University of Agriculture, Kyoto* 6, pp. 164–174.

Kudrjavtseva, E. (Cancer Research Centre, Moscow), Petrash, E. (All-Russia Institute for Genetics) and Sokolova, G. (Moscow State University) (1995) *The Tragedy of the St Nicholas Church in Kovda and Problems of Restoration of Russian Wooden Architectural Monuments*. Unpublished report.

Langberg, H. (1975) *Venezia-charteret om bevaringsarbejde*. København: Fonden for dansk Bygningskultur.

Larsen, K. E. and Marstein, N. (eds) (1992) *International Symposium on Fire Protection of Historic Buildings and Towns. Risør, Norway, 12–14 September 1990. Symposium Proceedings*. Trondheim: Tapir Publishers.

Larsen, K. E. (1994) *Architectural Preservation in Japan*. Trondheim/Paris: Tapir Publishers/ICOMOS International Wood Committee.

Larsen, K. E. and Marstein, N. (eds) (1994a) *ICOMOS International Wood Committee. 8th International Symposium. Kathmandu, Patan and Bhaktapur, Nepal, 23–25 November 1992. Proceedings*. Trondheim: Tapir Publishers.

Larsen, K. E. and Marstein, N. (eds) (1994b) *Conference on Authenticity in Relation to the World Heritage Convention. Preparatory Workshop. Bergen, Norway, 31 January – 2 February 1994. Workshop Proceedings*. Trondheim: Tapir Publishers.

Larsen, K. E. (ed.) (1995) *Nara Conference on Authenticity/Conference de Nara sur l'Authenticité. Proceedings/Compte-rendu.* Trondheim/Tokyo: Tapir Publishers/Agency for Cultural Affairs, Japan.

Lee, I. D. G. (1970) Testing for Safety in Timber Structures. In: *Symposium on Non-destructive Testing of Concrete and Timber.* London: The Institution of Civil Engineers, pp. 115–118.

Lowenthal, D. (1992) Counterfeit Art: Authentic Fakes. *International Journal of Cultural Property,* 1, 79–103.

Luong, M. P. (1996) Infrared Thermography of Damaged Wood. In: *10th International Symposium on Nondestructive Testing of Wood. Lausanne, Switzerland, 26-28 August 1996. Proceedings.* Lausanne: Presses polytechniques et universitaires romandes, pp. 175–185.

Macgregor, J. E. M. (1991) *Strengthening Timber Floors.* London: Society for the Protection of Ancient Buildings. Technical pamphlet 2.

Mader, G. T. (1989) Zur Frage der denkmalpflegerischen Konzeption bei technischen Sicherungsmassnahmen. In: *Konzeptionen. Möglichkeiten und Grenzen denkmalpflegerischer Massnahmen.* Arbeitshefte des Sonderforschungsbereiches 315 'Erhalten historisch bedeutsamer Bauwerke', 9. Universität Karlsruhe, pp. 23–52.

Mader, G. T. (1991) Methoden und Verfahren zur Erhaltung historischer Holzbaukonstruktionen. In: *Untersuchungen an Material und Konstruktionen historischer Bauwerke.* Arbeitshefte des Sonderforschungsbereiches 315 'Erhalten historisch bedeutsamer Bauwerke', 10. Universität Karlsruhe, pp. 57–68.

Mainstone, R. (1975) *Developments in Structural Form.* London: Allen Lane.

Marstein, N. (1992) Fire Protection of Historic Buildings and Towns in Norway. In: *International Symposium on Fire Protection of Historic Buildings and Towns. Risør, Norway, 12–14 September 1990. Symposium Proceedings* (K. E. Larsen and N. Marstein, eds). Trondheim: Tapir Publishers, pp. 11–23.

Mennim, A. M. (1988) Guidelines for the Conservation of Timber Structures. *Association for Studies in the Conservation of Historic Buildings Transactions,* XIII.

Mills, E. D. (ed.) (1994) *Building Maintenance and Preservation.* Oxford: Butterworth–Heinemann.

Ministero per i Beni Culturali e Ambientali; Archivio di Stato di Venezia (1987) *Boschi della Serenissima – utilizzo e tutela. Mostra documentaria, 25 luglio – 4 ottobre 1987.* Venezia: Archivio di Stato di Venezia.

Myhre, L. (1996) *Learning from the Built Heritage on the way Towards a Sustainable Development.* Oslo: Norwegian Building Research Institute. Project Report 198–1996.

Neuwirth, F. (1987) Values of a Monument in a New World. In: *ICOMOS 8th General Assembly and International Symposium. Symposium Papers, Volume 1.* Washington, DC: US ICOMOS, pp. 127–133.

Parham, R. A. and Gray, R. L. (1984) Formation and Structure of Wood. In: *The Chemistry of Solid Wood,* Advances in Chemistry Series 207 (R. Rowell, ed.). Washington, DC: American Chemical Society, pp. 3–56.

Peterken, G. F. (1996) *Natural Woodland. Ecology and Conservation in Northern Temperate Regions.* Cambridge: Cambridge University Press.

Petzet, M. (1995) 'In the full richness of their authenticity' – The Test of Authenticity and the New Cult of Monuments. In: *Nara Conference on Authenticity/Conference de Nara sur l'Authenticité. Proceedings/Compte-rendu* (K. E. Larsen, ed.). Trondheim/Tokyo: Tapir Publishers/Agency for Cultural Affairs, Japan, pp. 85–99.

Phleps, H. (1942) *Holzbaukunst der Blockbau. Ein Fachbuch zur Erziehung werkgerechten Gestaltens in Holz.* Karlsruhe: Fachblattverlag Dr. Albert Bruder.

Ponnert, H. (1994) Traditionella byggnadsmaterial – har de en framtid? *Kulturmiljövård,* 2/3, 3–5.

Ponnert, H. and Sjömar, P. (1993) Trä och träbyggnadskonst. *Nordisk arkitekturforskning,* 1, 23–39.

Ponnert, H. and Sjömar, P. (1994a) Bilat eller sågat restaureringsvirke. *Kulturmiljövård,* 1, 19–25.

Ponnert, H. and Sjömar, S. (1994b) Trä och träbyggnadskonst – material, byggnadsteknik, hantverk och restaurering. *Kulturmiljövård,* 1, 26–30.

Rodgers, W. A. (1997) Patterns of loss of forest biodiversity – a global perspective. In: *Proceedings of the XI World Forestry Congress, 13–22 October 1997, Antalya,* vol. 2, pp. 23–39.

Salaün, C. (1995) L'application de la technique dite du 'bois percé' et de ses dérivés dans le domain de la restauration. In: *Le bois dans l'architecture.* Paris: Picard, pp. 279–282.

Salwasser, H, MacCleery, D.W. and Snellgrove, T.A. (1990) An Ecosystem Perspective on Sustainable Forestry and New Directions for the U.S. National Forest System. In: *Defining Sustainable Forestry* (H. Aplet, N. Johnson, J.T. Olson and V. A. Samle, eds). Washington, DC: Island Press, pp. 44–89.

Samidi, Sadirin and Subyantoro (1993) Traditional Conservation of Wooden Carved Houses of Kudus (Indonesia) In: *Fourth Seminar on the Conservation of Asian Cultural Heritage. Traditional Materials and Techniques in Conservation. October 31 – November 3 1993, Nara.* Nara: Nara National Cultural Properties Research Institute, pp. 117–138.

Sandin, Y. (1996) *Verkningssätt hos äldre trätakstolar*

i svenska kyrkor. Göteborg: Chalmers tekniska högskola. Institutionen för form och teknik.

Sekino, M. (1978) Principles of Conservation and Restoration Regarding Wooden Buildings in Japan. In: *International Symposium on the Conservation and Restoration of Cultural Property – Conservation of Wood.* Tokyo: Tokyo National Research Institute of Cultural Properties, pp. 127–142.

Smart, B. (1972) How to reidentify the ship of Theseus. *Analysis,* 32, 145–148.

Stalnaker, J. J. and Harris, E. C. (1989) *Structural Design in Wood.* New York: Van Nostrand Reinhold.

Stipe, R. E. (1990) ICOMOS: A Quarter of a Century. Symposium sub-theme the Venice Charter. Prepared by US/ICOMOS. In: *ICOMOS Ninth General Assembly and International Symposium. Symposium Papers.* Lausanne: ICOMOS Switzerland, pp. 407–424.

Susmel, L. (1994) *I Rovereti di Pianura della Serenissima.* Padova: Cooperativa Libraria Editrice Università di Padova.

Troelsgård, E. (1995) Reparation af Tagværker. *Information om bygningsbevaring* 050690-16. København: Miljøministeriet, Planstyrelsen.

UNESCO (1972) *Convention Concerning the Protection of the World Cultural and Natural Heritage.* Adopted by the General Conference at its seventeenth session. Paris, 16 November 1972.

UNESCO (1988) *Operational Guidelines for the Implementation of the World Heritage Convention.* Intergovernmental Committee for the Protection of the World Cultural and Natural Heritage.

Vreim, H. (1948) *Laftehus.* Oslo: Noregs Boklag.

Weaver, M. (1993) *Conserving Historic Buildings.* New York: John Wiley & Sons.

Weiss, N. R. and Gale, F. R. (1983) Wood Extractives as Wood Preservatives. In: *Conservation of Wooden Monuments. Proceedings of the ICOMOS Wood Committee IVth International Symposium, Canada, June 1982* (R. O. Byrne, J. Lemire, J. Oberlander *et al.,* eds). Ottawa: ICOMOS Canada and the Heritage Canada Foundation, pp.138–142.

Whittaker, M. M., Kersten, P. J., Nakamura, N., Sanders-Loehr, J, Schweizer, E. S. and Whittaker, J. W. (1996) Glyoxal Oxidase from *Phanerochaete chrysosporium* is a New Radical-Copper Oxidase. *Journal of Biological Chemistry,* 2, 681–687.

Wyss, A. (1994) Kleiner Katechismus – Denkmalpflege als moralische Frage. *Die Denkmalpflege,* 2, 123–128.

Zhong, Y. and Chen, Y. (eds) (1986) *History and Development of Chinese Architecture.* Compiled by the Institute of the History of Natural Sciences, Chinese Academy of Sciences. Beijing: Science Press.

Index